CAT F

To Tommy Willborn
With me are congratulations
on your achievements,
and with best
wishes for your
continuing advancements
in life — may this
be as successful as
you were while a boy
in England, with the
slant on the tally-ho horn!

Your devoted Uncle
Ralph W. Yarborough

**Yarborough
OF
TEXAS**

Washington-on-the-Brazos
Feb. 2, 1973.

Yarborough
OF
TEXAS

By William G. Phillips

Published by

acropolis books

Washington, D. C. 20009

THE CONGRESSIONAL LEADERSHIP SERIES

Volume No. 1
HOW A SENATOR MAKES GOVERNMENT WORK—METCALF OF MONTANA
BY Richard D. Warden

Volume No. 2
LIBERAL LEADER IN THE HOUSE—FRANK THOMPSON, JR.
by Augusta Elliott Wilson

Volume No. 3
THE GOLDEN VOICE OF THE SENATE—DIRKSEN OF ILLINOIS
by Annette Culler Penney

Volume No. 4
YARBOROUGH OF TEXAS
by William G. Phillips

ACROPOLIS BOOKS
Colortone Building, 2400 17th St., N.W.
Washington, D. C. 20009

CONGRESSIONAL LEADERSHIP SERIES—VOLUME NO. 4

Printed in the United States of America by
Colortone Creative Printing
Washington, D. C. 20009

Type set in Bodoni (Compugraphic)
by Colortone Typographic Division, Inc.

Design by Design and Art Studio 2400, Inc.

Library of Congress Catalog Number 74-107544

Standard Book Number (Cloth) 87491-124-9
                        (Paper) 87491-125-7

Contents

Introduction

The office walls in Senator Ralph W. Yarborough's Senate Office Building suite in Washington are lined with plaques and awards and warmly inscribed photographs of many of the political leaders of our time. The oldest decoration, however, is a framed enlargement of a paragraph clipped from the April 7, 1957, issue of the Austin *American Statesman*. It occupies the most prominent spot in the Senator's busy reception room. It has hung there since he was first elected a United States Senator from Texas in 1957. It reads:

> "A prominent local lobbyist stopped in at Ralph Yarborough's campaign headquarters on Congress Avenue on election night. Talking to newsmen at the Capitol, he spoke wonderingly of what he'd seen. 'It was fantastic,' he muttered, 'There wasn't a big shot down there! Nothing but people!' "

This subtle tribute helps explain why many refer to Ralph Yarborough as "the people's Senator" and why millions of Texans call him "my Senator." No higher compliment can be paid any elected official than such a possessive identification. It signifies a public servant's relationship with his fellow citizens that exemplifies the highest objectives of truly representative government, a personal bond of a nature that is becoming ever more difficult to maintain in our modern push-button society.

This book traces the early defeats and later triumphs in the colorful political career of one of the Nation's most distinguished public servants—Senator Ralph W. Yarborough. For over 15 years Yarborough has been the leader of the nationally-oriented Democrats in Texas—a party within a party. It concerns his astonishing versatility, his tireless work in the Senate in such wide-ranging legislative areas as education, health, conservation, labor, public works, agriculture, defense and myriad other fields. It describes Yarborough's profound impact on Texas politics and the force of his magnetic leadership that has unified Texas' diverse social, economic, and nationality groupings as no one else has been able to do.

His inspiring story provides insights into his broad new responsibilities as Chairman of the Senate Labor and Public Welfare Committee; he is Texas' first regular Senate Committee chairman since the late Tom Connally retired in 1953. Finally, the book highlights his significant legislative achievements on the national scene during the past 12 years. Although his major legislative victories such as the Cold War GI Bill and the Padre Island National Seashore are well known, probably relatively few realize how active and effective Yarborough has been in a score of areas. This book attempts to provide a comprehensive picture of Yarborough's almost incredible range of activities and interests. It looks ahead with high hope at the key role Chairman Yarborough is destined to play as America moves boldly with him into the decade of the 1970's.

As the late President John F. Kennedy said a month before his death:

"Ralph Yarborough speaks for Texas in the United States Senate, and he also speaks for our nation, and he speaks for progress for our people."

W.G.P.

Senate Labor & Public Welfare Committee

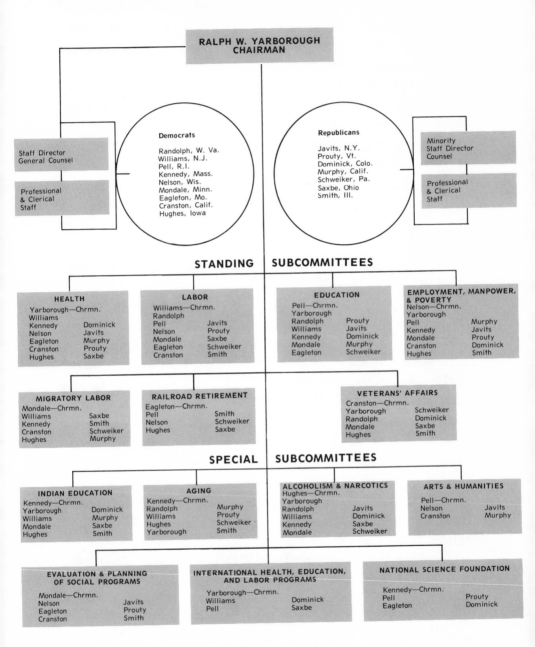

RALPH W. YARBOROUGH
CHAIRMAN

Staff Director
General Counsel

Professional
& Clerical
Staff

Democrats
Randolph, W. Va.
Williams, N.J.
Pell, R.I.
Kennedy, Mass.
Nelson, Wis.
Mondale, Minn.
Eagleton, Mo.
Cranston, Calif.
Hughes, Iowa

Republicans
Javits, N.Y.
Prouty, Vt.
Dominick, Colo.
Murphy, Calif.
Schweiker, Pa.
Saxbe, Ohio
Smith, Ill.

Minority
Staff Director
Counsel

Professional
& Clerical
Staff

STANDING | SUBCOMMITTEES

HEALTH
Yarborough—Chrmn.
Williams
Kennedy   Dominick
Nelson   Javits
Eagleton   Murphy
Cranston   Prouty
Hughes   Saxbe

LABOR
Williams—Chrmn.
Randolph
Pell   Javits
Nelson   Prouty
Mondale   Saxbe
Eagleton   Schweiker
Cranston   Smith

EDUCATION
Pell—Chrmn.
Yarborough
Randolph   Prouty
Williams   Javits
Kennedy   Dominick
Mondale   Murphy
Eagleton   Schweiker

EMPLOYMENT, MANPOWER, & POVERTY
Nelson—Chrmn.
Yarborough
Pell   Murphy
Kennedy   Javits
Mondale   Prouty
Cranston   Dominick
Hughes   Smith

MIGRATORY LABOR
Mondale—Chrmn.
Williams   Saxbe
Kennedy   Smith
Cranston   Schweiker
Hughes   Murphy

RAILROAD RETIREMENT
Eagleton—Chrmn.
Pell   Smith
Nelson   Schweiker
Hughes   Saxbe

VETERANS' AFFAIRS
Cranston—Chrmn.
Yarborough   Schweiker
Randolph   Dominick
Mondale   Saxbe
Hughes   Smith

SPECIAL | SUBCOMMITTEES

INDIAN EDUCATION
Kennedy—Chrmn.
Yarborough   Dominick
Williams   Murphy
Mondale   Saxbe
Hughes   Smith

AGING
Kennedy—Chrmn.
Randolph   Murphy
Williams   Prouty
Hughes   Schweiker
Yarborough   Smith

ALCOHOLISM & NARCOTICS
Hughes—Chrmn.
Yarborough
Randolph   Javits
Williams   Dominick
Kennedy   Saxbe
Mondale   Schweiker

ARTS & HUMANITIES
Pell—Chrmn.
Nelson   Javits
Cranston   Murphy

EVALUATION & PLANNING OF SOCIAL PROGRAMS
Mondale—Chrmn.
Nelson   Javits
Eagleton   Prouty
Cranston   Smith

INTERNATIONAL HEALTH, EDUCATION, AND LABOR PROGRAMS
Yarborough—Chrmn.
Williams   Dominick
Pell   Saxbe

NATIONAL SCIENCE FOUNDATION
Kennedy—Chrmn.
Pell   Prouty
Eagleton   Dominick

SENATOR RALPH W. YARBOROUGH OF TEXAS became Chairman of the Senate Labor and Public Welfare Committee in January, 1969. Its legislative jurisdiction touches programs that affect the lives of every American. Over the past two decades, the Committee has produced an abundance of national leaders. It has spawned two Presidents—John F. Kennedy and Richard M. Nixon as well as five Presidential contenders—Senators Humphrey, Goldwater, Taft, Thurmond and Robert F. Kennedy.

With the 91st Congress, Chairman Yarborough's Committee marks its 100th anniversary. It was initially established as the Committee on Education in January 1869, during the 41st Congress. Its chief architect was Senator Justin Morrill of Vermont, author of the historic Morrill Land Grant College Act seven years earlier while a member of the House of Representatives. A year later, the committee's jurisdiction was broadened and its name was changed to the Senate Education and Labor Committee. It carried this title until it became the Labor and Public Welfare Committee under the Legislative Reorganization Act of 1946.

Among the first Senators appointed to the new Education and Labor Committee in 1870 was Senator James W. Flanagan, a Texas Republican of the Reconstruction period. Flanagan became Chairman of the Committee in the 43rd Congress. In the next Congress he was succeeded by a former Texas Confederate General, Samuel B. Maxey. Democrat Maxey moved into Flanagan's former seat on the Senate Education and Labor Committee in December 1875. He served on the committee for eight years. Another well-known Texan, Senator Morris Sheppard of Texarkana, was a member of the committee in the late 1920's. Yarborough is only the fifth Texan to have served on the Committee during its 100-year history.

Charles Richard Yarborough, the Senator's father, was an East Texas pioneer family man and a staunch Democrat. He lived 11 days past his 100th birthday and was one of Ralph Yarborough's most vigorous campaigners and wisest advisers until the end. The Senator's grandfather, Harvey Yarborough, was County Coroner in Sumter County, Alabama and served as a First Lieutenant during the Mexican War. He moved the Yarborough clan to Texas and in 1861 organized the first infantry company from Smith County when Texas joined the Confederacy. There was a strong, traditional patriotic fervor in the Yarborough family, as in most old rural American families.

Texas Heritage

FOR WELL OVER A CENTURY, Henderson County in east Texas has been Yarborough country. Formed in 1846, it takes its name from J. Pinckney Henderson, first State Governor who later served as a United States Senator. Diversity of land, people, and products are its dominant characteristics.

The gently rolling hills are dotted with pines, ash, gum, hickory, and post oak. To the west, the Trinity River flows southward into Galveston Bay; to the east, the Neches River makes its way slowly to the Gulf of Mexico some 150 miles away. Henderson County's rich farmland produces a variety of crops—cotton, corn, melons, peanuts, tomatoes, potatoes and black-eyed peas, for which it is most famous.

The people are hardworking, industrious, economically and politically independent. Farmers, industrial and skilled workers, and the usual assortment of small businesses comprise the county's work force and commercial establishments.

Areas of heavy clay soil support brick, tile, and pottery plants. Small sawmills, furniture plants, dairy, beef cattle, canning and clothing industries add to the economic mix. Oil and gas wells on the landscape help give Henderson County the "Texas look."

Ralph Webster Yarborough was born in the town of Chandler (present population 627), some twelve miles west of Tyler. He was the seventh of eleven children of Charles Richard and Nannie Jane Yarborough, who, like their neighbors, prided themselves on traditional frontier self-reliance and independent thinking. The Yarborough family has a history of leadership in civic and public affairs. Ralph's father was Mayor, School Board President and Justice of the Peace in Chandler. His grandfather, Harvey Yarborough, led the first company of infantry from adjoining Smith County when Texas joined the Confederacy in 1861.

Legendary Heroes

Young Ralph became an avid student of history, an interest that has grown and matured. In the evenings after the day's chores were done, he sat in the family circle on the cool back gallery and learned about Thomas Jefferson, Madison, the Constitution, Andy Jackson's frontier democracy and his struggle against Nicholas Biddle and the National Bank; about Sam Houston, Stephen Austin the martyrs of the Alamo and Goliad, about San Jacinto and the founding of the Texas Republic.

He learned about the history of Henderson County, "training ground for statesmen." They included John H. Reagan, first judge of Henderson County, who had served in the cabinet of President Jefferson Davis. Reagan had served in the House of Representatives, both before and after the Civil War. He led the fight on railroad abuses and became a United States Senator from Texas. In Washington, he had helped write the Interstate Commerce Act and in 1891 became the first chairman of the Texas Railroad Commission.

Another county hero was the "Old Alcalde," Oran M. Roberts, a district judge who was elected Governor in 1878. During his two administrations, the University of Texas, Sam Houston State and Prarie View Colleges were established and a Statewide system of free public schools was begun. Roberts also served as Chief Justice of the Texas Supreme Court. Then there was "Howdy" Martin, Civil War hero in Hood's Brigade, who served as district attorney and as a Congressman.

East Texas is rich in the Populist tradition, which took the form of the Farmers' State Alliance and The People's Party during the 1880's and 1890's. Economic and political upheavals of the Reconstruction years had brought hardship and deprivation to many thousands of small farmers and workers. Prices of cotton, corn, and other basic commodities plummeted with the Panic in 1873 and dropped still lower in the following decade. Jobs were unsteady and wages poor.

The end of "carpetbag" rule in the 1870's had brought a return of more stable State and local government to Texas and other Southern States, but it was a virtual "one party" government dominated largely by bankers, merchants, large landholders and other commercial interests with little sympathy for the plight of the small farmer or the working man. When coupled with unscrupulous rate practices of the railroad "barons" and widespread vote-stealing and political corruption, the stage was set for an organized economic and political counterattack by frustrated and desperate citizens of the rural areas of Texas and other States of the South and Midwest. In some areas farmers joined forces with newly-organized urban workers' groups such as the Knights of Labor. They campaigned for reform of the banking laws, for a graduated income tax and for direct election of United States Senators; they advocated free coinage of silver, reforms in the railroad, and an end to corruption in business, in the conduct of elections, and in the affairs of government.

Agitation for reform spread and the Populist movement made some significant, although temporary, gains in a number of States. In Texas, People's Party candidates for Governor in 1892, 1894 and 1896 made strong races but could not succeed in winning control of the State government. Gradually, the two major parties undermined Populist appeal at the State and National levels by adopting many of their economic reforms and political objectives.

In Texas, a trust-busting Democratic reformer was elected Attorney General in 1886 and in 1891 became Governor, campaigning on an anti-monopoly platform. James S. Hogg, the "Great Commoner," was the first native Texan to serve as Governor. His strong beliefs and actions in preserving the public interest were to have a profound influence over Ralph Yarborough many years later. Young Ralph's father had tutored him on the accomplishments of the progressive administrations of Jim Hogg and those of Charles A. Culbertson and Thomas M. Campbell, who followed in Hogg's footsteps of economic and political reform that marked the turn of the century period in Texas history.

More than a generation later, Ralph Yarborough was to demonstrate just how well he had learned these lessons that were such an important part of his colorful Texas heritage.

The Yarborough family home in Chandler, Henderson County, was dedicated as a State Historical Building in December, 1966. The Senator (center) reads the historical marker in the front yard of the Yarborough home. His two brothers, Harvey J. Yarborough (left) and Donald Yarborough (right) are both attorneys who practice law in Dallas. The Yarborough family settled in East Texas during the period of the Texas Republic, more than 125 years ago. Yarborough's mother, Nannie Jane Spear Yarborough, was a descendant of the Walton family of Georgia that furnished a signer of the Declaration of Independence. Twenty-nine Yarboroughs served in the Continental army during the Revolutionary War.

Senator Ralph Webster Yarborough, Texas' Senior Senator, now lives in Austin. Chairman of the influential Senate Labor & Public Welfare Committee, he bears major responsibility for Federal-State programs that provided over $2.6 billion in Federal funds to Texas during the past Fiscal year. First elected to the Senate in April, 1957, he is now completing his second full six-year term. His powerful position on the Appropriations Committee, his seniority, and his record of legislative accomplishment for the people of Texas and the Nation combine to make him one of America's leading public officials.

Preparing for Public Leadership

THROUGHOUT HIS YEARS OF INFORMAL family training in the history and traditions of Texas, public affairs, and the integrity of public office, Ralph Yarborough attended the public schools in Chandler, where he played on the basketball team. His father had a burning ambition that all of his three sons become lawyers. He lived to see that ambition fulfilled. When he died in 1964, eleven days after his 100th birthday, Charles Richard Yarborough had two sons, Donald and H. J., who were both practicing law in Dallas. Son Ralph was by then serving his eighth year in the United States Senate after a distinguished career as an attorney, Assistant Attorney General of Texas, and district judge.

Ralph attended high school in nearby Tyler and was active on the debate team. One of his schoolmates was "the girl next door," Opal Warren, who was later to become Mrs. Ralph Yarborough and one of his most valuable assets in political as well as personal life. He graduated from Tyler High School in 1919, eager to pursue his education.

Soon thereafter, Congressman Jim Young of Kaufman County appointed young Ralph to the U.S. Military Academy at West Point. It took him only one year to decide that despite the high caliber of the educational opportunities afforded at the Academy, an Army career was not his life goal. He resigned and returned home to Chandler, where he took a job with a threshing crew, working across the wheat fields of Kansas and Oklahoma.

Young Teacher

The seventeen-year-old Yarborough embarked on a teaching career in one-room schools in nearby Martin Springs and Delta. From this rewarding experience can be

17

traced the interest that culminated in his leadership in the Senate on every major education bill enacted by Congress after his election in 1957. He enrolled in Sam Houston State College in Huntsville in 1921 and sandwiched studies between his teaching duties.

When he turned eighteen, young Yarborough decided it was time for him to see the world and to pursue his education in Europe. He worked his way across the Atlantic via cattle-boat from New Orleans, unsuccessfully sought entrance to the Sorbonne in Paris, and finally wound up in Berlin. He was hired as Assistant Secretary of the American Chamber of Commerce, studied German and entered the Stendhal Academy. He worked and studied in Germany for a year and then headed home to Texas via England, working his passage to New York as a handler of a shipment of horses on a British merchantman.

In the fall of 1923 he decided on a career in law and enrolled at the University of Texas Law School in Austin. He worked to pay his tuition and expenses—waited on tables in a boarding house for two years, worked part-time as a librarian when in school and as a construction worker in the Texas oil fields. He also enlisted in the 36th Division of the Texas National Guard. It was a decision that was to become important when the attack on Pearl Harbor plunged the nation into war. Yarborough was an outstanding student and in 1927 he graduated from the law school with highest honors. Soon after, he joined the El Paso law firm of Turney, Burges, Culwell & Pollard.

Texas Lawyer

The following year he returned to East Texas long enough to marry his childhood sweetheart, Opal Warren. After high school, Opal had attended Texas State College for Women, where she received a degree in Home Economics with high honors and had taught school in Clarksville, Texas and in Pine Bluff, Arkansas. Back in El

The Senator's charming wife, Opal Warren Yarborough, was a high school schoolmate and Ralph's childhood sweetheart. Their son Richard and his wife Ann have two daughters, Clare and Elizabeth. Richard is, like his famous dad, an attorney. He now serves as a Commissioner of the Indian Claims Commission in Washington. The Yarboroughs are shown here at a reception sponsored by the National Association of Letter Carriers.

During the 1958 Senate campaign, Senator Yarborough visited his old high school in Tyler, Texas. He is shown here inspecting historic voter registration records at the school.

Paso, Yarborough pursued his law career with new energy, specializing in land and water rights law. He became a recognized authority in these complex fields. His son, Dick, was born in 1931 in Austin.

The election of Herbert Hoover to the Presidency, the stock market crash, and the ensuing depression brought general economic collapse and hardship to the people of Texas as well as the rest of the country. Yarborough's long-time interest in politics quickened, and in 1930 he entered the arena to campaign for the brother of a law school friend who was running for Attorney General. The eventual winner was the opponent, James V. Allred.

First Public Office

Soon after taking office, Attorney General Allred observed and was impressed by the way the young attorney from El Paso handled himself in presenting arguments on a land matter before the Attorney General in Austin. Despite the campaign activities on behalf of his opponent, Allred appointed Yarborough as an Assistant Attorney General. He was assigned the responsibility of the State's Permanent School Fund, which had a total investment fund of more than $40 million. Yarborough also had legal responsibility for the University of Texas Permanent Fund, where he could make full use of his land law knowledge to protect the public interest.

In the Yates Oil Field case he won a judgment of more than $1 million for the Permanent School Fund, at that time the second largest money judgment ever collected by the state of Texas. He established the State's interest in oil and gas and bonus rental income from 3.9 million acres of land in a suit involving the Magnolia Petroleum Company. He authored an opinion asserting State title to tidelands and advised the State Land Commissioner to issue leases. The revenue obtained from this action helped pioneer a new source of funds for improving the Texas public schools. In later years a demogogic opponent was to distort Yarborough's tidelands position when it became a national issue in the 1952 campaign. Yarborough also drafted the first underground water conservation law enacted in the State; conservation of our priceless natural resources has been one of his major areas of legislative accomplishment ever since.

During this hectic period, major changes of far reaching importance were taking place in America. Amid economic chaos, fear and uncertainty, the clear voice of Franklin D. Roosevelt carried across the land. He offered new hope and confidence to the people of the country and restored faith in our democratic institutions. The New Deal of FDR and his Vice Presidential running-mate "Cactus Jack" Garner swept into office, carrying with it a Democratic Congress in which other famous Texans—Sam Rayburn, Maury Maverick and Senator Tom Connally were to play leading roles. Soon the famous "100 days" of sweeping economic reform and emergency relief legislation began to take hold and America moved back from the precipice of total economic collapse and political anarchy.

In Texas the famous Miriam "Ma" Ferguson, the State's first woman governor elected in 1925, was elected for a second two year term in 1932. An amendment to the State Constitution during her administration authorized $20 million in "bread bonds" to help feed hungry Texans during the depths of the depression.

Reform vs. Reaction

In the Hogg tradition Jimmie Allred as Attorney General had ushered in a new era of vigorous reform in which Ralph Yarborough had played a leading part. In 1934 Allred ran for Governor and was elected as a strong partner of Roosevelt's in bringing progressive State government to the people of Texas. Part of this Federal-State team was a young Congressional assistant named Lyndon B. Johnson, who became director of the National Youth Administration in Texas.

Governor Allred instituted old-age pensions, a retirement system for teachers and state employees, and other

22

important measures. But his progressive program incurred the wrath of the entrenched and powerful economic interests who likewise fought FDR, the New Deal and the re-awakened trade union movement. In the 1936 election these forces of reaction formed the forerunner of later "Dixiecrat" and "Shivercrat" organizations. The group was called "Constitutional Democrats of Texas"; but both Allred and Roosevelt won overwhelming victories in Texas as FDR swept to his landslide re-election. However, the fight between the forces of progress and reaction was just beginning.

After Allred became Governor, Yarborough opened a law office in Austin and lectured on land law at the University of Texas Law School. He continued his support of public interest projects, working with rural groups to help bring needed electric power to farms under the newly-enacted Rural Electrification Act. More than twenty years later, Yarborough was working in the Senate to improve REA services to rural families in Texas and the Nation. He was a member of the board of directors of the Lower Colorado River Authority, where his knowledge of water and conservation law helped in the planning of a series of dams on the Colorado that have since provided water, power, flood control, and recreational benefits to two generations of Texans.

Judge Yarborough

Governor Allred appointed Yarborough as judge of the 53rd District Court in 1936 to fill a vacancy. He was elected to a four-year term. During three of his five years on the bench, he was the presiding judge of the Third Judicial District, comprising 33 counties in Central Texas. Judge Yarborough's genuine concern for people has always been the guiding principle of his long years of public service. On the bench his vigorous protection of the rights of all citizens, his dedication to justice and human dignity won him new respect and added to his growing stature as a public official.

He was elected President of the Travis County Bar Association and was active in community and church affairs.

Campaign Trail

By 1938 Yarborough was convinced that he could best serve the people of Texas and carry on the progressive policies of Allred by seeking the office of Attorney General, traditional springboard to the Governor's Mansion. He took leave from the bench and launched an exhausting Statewide campaign in the old family car on a shoestring budget. It was the typical kind of Yarborough campaign for which he has become famous—county fairs and courthouse steps—handshaking and personal contact.

Yarborough lost his first campaign for state elective office to a popular, All-American football quarterback from Southern Methodist University named Gerry Mann. But it was valuable political experience for young Yarborough and won for him a host of friends and supporters who have repeatedly demonstrated their confidence and loyalty over the years.

After six subsequent Statewide campaigns for Governor and Senator, Yarborough still firmly believes that the voters of Texas have the basic right to meet the candidate and to judge him on a personal basis; to grab his hand and to look him in the eye. He mistrusts the modern "hoopla" of a managed, public relations oriented campaign with its phony cathode images of candidates as projected by the mass medium of television.

Two decades had provided Ralph Yarborough with unique and broad types of experience, all of which helped to shape the qualities of leadership, integrity, legal knowledge, political judgment and human compassion that make up the ideal attributes for public service. The Japanese attack on Pearl Harbor brought to Yarborough the opportunity for another type of service to his State and Nation, as it did to millions of other Americans.

Yarborough volunteered for the Army soon after the outbreak of World War II. His year of military training at the Academy and his hitch in the Texas National Guard gave him a head start. After completing his Judge Advocate General Corps training, he was commissioned as a Captain and assigned to duty in the Pentagon in Washington. But a desk job was not for Ralph Yarborough. He requested combat service overseas and was transferred to the 97th Division, which saw action as part of the First Army in the Rhineland as the powerful Allied armies raced across France to attack Hitler's Germany. The 97th was subsequently shifted to General George Patton's Third Army, where it spearheaded the drive to liberate Czechoslovakia. The Nazi surrender in May 1945 brought the redeployment of the 97th Division to join Allied forces in the Pacific for the impending attack on Japan. But final Japanese capitulation and formal surrender on the deck of the battleship "Missouri" came as Lt. Colonel Yarborough was headed across the Pacific.

The Philippines were his first stop and then on to Yokohama, Japan, under General Douglas MacArthur's command as a military government officer. Yarborough and the 97th were assigned to govern central Honshu Province—one-seventh of the land area and population of the country. His knowledge and experience in government, law, and his abiding concern for people—whatever their race, creed, or nationality—helped bring stable, more democratic government to the defeated enemy.

Yarborough's military government experience also provided him with new insights into the postwar needs and problems of his native Texas. When he finally returned home in May 1946, his wartime military government experience, plus his years of training as a teacher, lawyer, judge and Assistant Attorney General brought new opportunities for public service that were to consume much of the next decade of Ralph Yarborough's career.

3
Texas Politics

TO UNDERSTAND PROPERLY THE ROLE of Ralph Yarborough as a Congressional leader and a moving force in the Senate of the United States, one must examine the way politics works in Texas.

Generalizations lead to oversimplifications. Both are particularly dangerous in politics. There is no question, however, that politics, as practiced in Texas' 254 counties, dozen major cities, hundred smaller cities and in its vast rural areas, is exceedingly complex. At times many of the 11 million Texans would probably agree that it could be called confusing or even chaotic—at the least volatile.

Anatomy of Texas Politics

Eminent political scientists, psychologists, sociologists, anthropologists and even apologists have tried to explain the Texas ballot-box phenomena. They have struggled to find some logical pattern that would apply to Texas' voting behavior over the past 50 years. What rationale could motivate the historic Texas election victories for such contrasting candidates as "Pa" and "Ma" Ferguson, Dan Moody, Herbert Hoover, Franklin D. Roosevelt, "Pappy" O'Daniel, Coke Stevenson, Lyndon Johnson, Harry Truman, Allan Shivers, Dwight Eisenhower, John F. Kennedy, Ralph Yarborough, John Tower, Hubert Humphrey and John Connally? Do the estimated 4 million registered voters in Texas have political dyslexia or is there some thread of conscious consistency that can be followed to some predictable conclusion?

27

Yarborough chats with another famous Texan, the late "Cactus Jack" Garner. Garner served two terms as Vice President of the United States under President Franklin D. Roosevelt and was a former Speaker of the U.S. House of Representatives, who endorsed Yarborough for both gubernatorial and senatorial races.

Perhaps the most logical analysis explaining the underlying forces in Texas is that of a distinguished political scientist, the late V. O. Key, Jr. Twenty years ago in his book *Southern Politics* he linked Texas political behavior with the State's economic power bases. He observed in Texas that "the changes of nine decades have weakened the heritage of southern traditionalism, revolutionized the economy, and made Texas more western than southern." He went on to point out:

"The Lone Star State is concerned about money and how to make it, about oil and sulphur and gas, about cattle and dust storms and irrigation, about cotton and banking and Mexicans."

Key astutely described what was to become the political and economic battleground of Ralph Yarborough in the next decade:

"Texans are coming to be concerned broadly about what government ought and ought not to do. In our times the grand issues of politics almost invariably turn on what extent shall wealth and power, corporate or personal, be restrained for the protection of the defenseless? What services shall the government perform? Who shall pay for them?"

"In Texas," Key predicted, "the vague outlines of a politics are emerging in which irrelevancies are pushed into the background and people divide broadly along liberal and conservative lines." He explained that one of the basic reasons for this economic determinism in Texas politics is "the personal insecurity of men suddenly made rich who are fearful lest they lose wealth." Key explained:

"In 40 years a new-rich class has arisen from the exploitation of natural resources in a gold rush atmosphere . . . men have built huge fortunes from scratch. Imbued with faith in individual self-reliance and unschooled in social responsibilities of wealth, many of these men have been more sensitive than a

Pennsylvania manufacturer to the policies of the Roosevelt and Truman Administrations."

Thus, Key concluded in his 1949 analysis that "the confluence of the anxieties of the newly rich and the repercussions of the New Deal in Texas pushed politics into a battle of conservatives versus liberals, terms of common usage in political discourse in the State."

Yarborough vs. Machine—1952

Ralph Yarborough described the situation more bluntly when he took the stump in his first up-hill fight for Governor against the conservative machine of Allan Shivers in 1952. He climbed into the family car, filled the gas tank, and went to the people of Texas—to the courthouse steps, to the fields, and to the Main Streets of villages and towns across the State. He hammered home these truths: (1) the State government was in the hands of a machine that favored a few wealthy corporations and special interests at the expense of the people of Texas; (2) the machine was corrupting the democratic process and destroying the Democratic party; and finally (3) the machine was fiscally corrupt in the handling of public funds.

Yarborough was a gubernatorial candidate against Shivers in 1952 by an accident of political fate. When he returned from World War II, politics was far from his mind. He resumed the practice of law in Austin, joined the American Legion and the Veterans of Foreign Wars, became active again in civic affairs and devoted as much time as possible to his family—wife, Opal, and son, Dick, who was then in high school.

He represented the Texas State Teachers Association and became a member of the Texas State Board of Law Examiners. His interest in the tidelands oil issue was reawakened when the Supreme Court ruled that Federal, rather than State claims to the off-shore lands was paramount. Having written the first legal opinion supporting the

Campaigning is a family affair for the Yarboroughs. The Senator believes in personal communication with the voters and in the importance of the old fashioned, hand-shaking type of campaign. He is shown here during a race for Governor with his late father and his wife, Opal. Yarborough has personally campaigned in each of Texas' 254 counties.

Texas' independent rural voters have been Ralph Yarborough's most loyal and reliable supporters in all of his campaigns. He likes nothing better than the opportunity to meet and discuss important issues and problems face-to-face with Texans on Main Streets, farms and ranches. The questioning voter is one of the challenges that Yarborough most enjoys.

Texas claim in 1931, Yarborough plunged into the controversy as a member of the executive committee of the Texas Property Defense Association. He also became a director of the Statewide Tidelands Committee.

Early in 1952 Yarborough was seriously considering running for Attorney General, not Governor. He put out feelers among friends, asking for their advice and counsel. Soon after, he was stopped in the corridor of the State Capitol by a prominent Texan who told him that the next Attorney General had already been selected and that it was useless for him to run. This was the Shivers machine at work. Yarborough asked himself and his close friends an obvious question: Was this the democracy that they had fought to preserve in World War II? How could a few wealthy, powerful individuals exercises such a degree of political and economic control over the destiny of an entire State and its people?

His Henderson County heritage and his dedication to principle gave the clear-cut answer. Yarborough would fight—whatever the cost, win or lose. He began to plan his campaign for Attorney General. He sought to persuade others to consider the race for Governor in an all-out, coordinated campaign against the Shivers machine. He called out his own political "machine"—the scores of immediate relatives in the Yarborough family, concentrated throughout East Texas and across the State.

Ralph Yarborough soon found that where he had encountered offhand discouragement of his candidacy, others were subjected to naked threats. Wherever he went he found that civic and business leaders, whom he had regarded as potential supporters, had received telephone calls warning them against any involvement in the Yarborough campaign. One corporate executive was threatened with the loss of his job; another businessman was reminded of an outstanding inventory loan; an insurance man was warned about the risk of antagonizing State regulatory agencies. This pattern of "either-or" economic pressure against potential Yarborough backers took many forms, all quite pervasive.

Shocked and angered by the dire implications of such unchecked economic and political power on the future of democratic government, Yarborough made a momentous decision. He returned home to Austin and announced his candidacy for Governor. He said:

> "If I'm going to fight an organized machine, a conspiracy against democracy—then I might as well buck the lead dog."

The "lead dog" was the darling of the Texas "Regulars" who had fought Roosevelt's nomination and re-election in 1944, had bucked Lyndon Johnson in his bid for the Senate in 1948, and had supported the Dixiecrat ticket against President Truman that same year. Governor Allan Shivers was indeed a formidable opponent.

Yarborough was, moreover, ill-prepared to wage a winning campaign against the powerful, well-financed "Shivercrat" forces. As a political pragmatist, he knew his chances were indeed slim. Economic threats imposed on potential contributors made campaign funds scarce.

Moreover, 1952 was the most unpropitious year possible to wage a campaign of affirmance of the Roosevelt-Truman tradition. In one of politic's cyclical movements, the Texas mood was swinging toward the hero-General to stop the unpopular "Truman's War." But what Ralph Yarborough lacked in organization, money and literature was more than made up by his determination. He took his case to the people and waged a vigorous, hard-hitting campaign against the Shivers machine and its oppressive influence over Texas and its people. It was a lonely race. The press either ignored his charges of corruption leveled at the machine or distorted his position. He had no organization, little money and minimum exposure in many key areas of the State. He received partial labor endorsement and almost half a million Texas voters marked their ballots for Yarborough on election day—more than even his most optimistic supporters had thought possible. He carried 21 counties, one less than he had won in his race for Attorney General 14 years earlier.

Shivers had won by promising to support the Democratic nominees for President and Vice President. But in September, 1952 Shivers led the State Democratic Executive Committee to reverse that position and to unanimously endorse the Republican ticket and he actively campaigned for the Eisenhower-Nixon team. In exchange, Shivers was also given the Republican nomination and was re-elected Governor without opposition.

In 1952 Yarborough had fought a holding action against corruption and reaction of the Shivers machine. In 1954 he set out to win and began planning his campaign soon after the 1952 defeat. His growing number of loyal supporters throughout the State went to work to rebuild the loyalist wing of the Democratic party.

Yarborough Coalition

The elements of the "Yarborough coalition" began to take shape and the division between Yarborough loyalists and Shivercrat forces became more pronounced, just as political scientist Key had predicted. But political labels, then as now, are often misleading. Yarborough and his supporters shared a basic belief in the strength of truly democratic government. They abhorred special interest dictation of human destiny and were dedicated to the fight against political extremists, racial discrimination, anti-union policies and against corruption in business and in government.

Yarborough counted on the support of small farmers all the way from his native East Texas to the Panhandle; he sought the votes of working people in small factories and in large industrial plants of major cities; he carried his case to the field workers of large industrial farm complexes and employees of urban retail establishments. Others in the Yarborough coalition included small businessmen; leaders of

35

Yarborough and

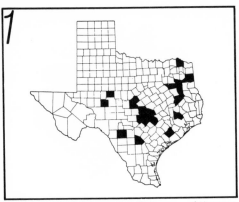

1938—First Democratic Primary—Attorney
General: Led in 22 Counties with 220,964 votes

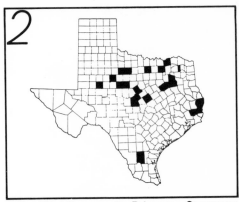

1952—First Democratic Primary—Governor:
Led in 21 Counties with 488,345 votes

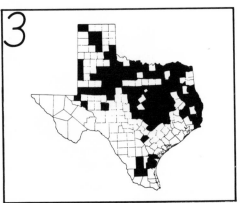

1954—First Democratic Primary—Governor:
Led in 116 Counties with 645,994 votes

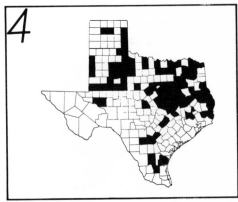

1954—Second (Run-off) Democratic
Primary—Governor: Led in 95 Counties with
683,132 votes

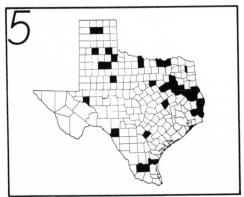

1956—First Democratic Primary—Governor:
Led in 34 Counties with 463,416 votes

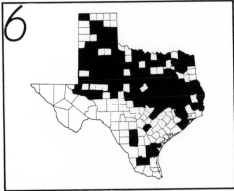

1956—Second (Run-off) Democratic Primary—Governor: Led in 146 Counties with
694,830 votes

The TexasVoters

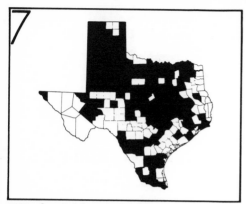

1957—Special Senatorial Election: Led in 172 Counties with 364,605 votes

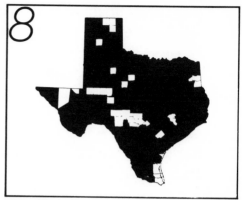

1958—First Democratic Primary—Senator: Led in 223 Counties with 761,511 votes

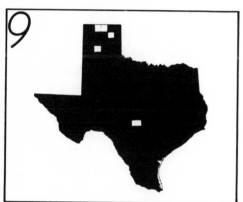

1958—November General Election—Senator: Led in 249 Counties with 587,030 votes

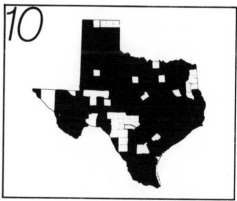

1964—First Democratic Primary—Senator: Led in 213 Counties with 905,011 votes

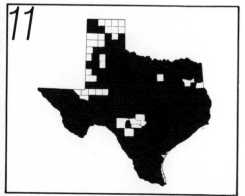

1964—November General Election—Senator: Led in 220 Counties with 1,463,958 votes

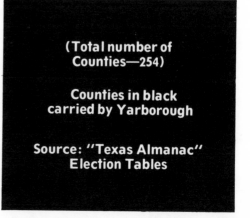

(Total number of Counties—254)

Counties in black carried by Yarborough

Source: "Texas Almanac" Election Tables

the campus intellectual community, heads of labor unions, teachers' organizations and other professional groups; the poor, underprivileged, and exploited—Americans of Mexican descent, Negroes and other minority groups. The broad-based coalition was made up of the well-springs of economic and political vitality that have characterized Texas' remarkable midcentury growth and accomplishment. Formation of this coalition was greatly helped by the amazingly public rejection of these groups Shivers & company would make. Basically, it was the same base of support that makes up the Democratic Party nationally.

Yarborough vs. Corruption—1954

The campaign against Yarborough for Governor in 1954 was marked by mudslinging and character assassination that reflected the fear and desperation of Yarborough's opponents. Senator Joe McCarthy was at the peak of his influence. Democrats in many parts of the country were subjected to similar smear tactics. But Yarborough ignored the slander and falsehoods against him. He continued to wage his vigorous handshaking, barnstorming, personal campaign on an 18 hour-a-day schedule that took him into every corner of the State. The lack of adequate campaign funds was as always, a problem.

Yarborough hit hard at the corrupting influences in the State government and outlined a program to rid the State of its economic and political parasites. He fought to restore integrity and progressive government to Texas in the Hogg-Allred tradition. He refused to permit his supporters to reply in kind to his opponent's smear-sheet efforts. Again, most of the Texas press either ignored him or glossed over his charges.

During the campaign, Yarborough said over and over:

"To a political machine, the object is power, first, last, and always. And principles are just a propaganda device. . . . A democrat tries to win friends. . . . A

38

Texas' political campaigns are personal experiences for Ralph Yarborough. Rallies such as this are typical, complete with entertainment, refreshments and good fellowship. Yarborough is the most indefatigible campaigner in Texas' history.

political machine uses methods which are a tip-off to its goal—to destroy opposition, to destroy discussion—to rule by leaving the people no choice."

The Eisenhower glow was wearing off. One of Yarborough's best issues was his loyalty to the Democratic party versus Shivers' 1952 betrayal of it. His vigorous campaign gave the people of Texas a choice, although many of them were still disfranchised by the poll tax and rigged voter registration laws which discouraged political participation.

In the first primary the results were:

Allan Shivers	668,913
Ralph Yarborough	645,994
"Cyclone" Davis	16,254
J. J. Holmes	19,591

In the run-off election Yarborough lost to Governor Shivers by a margin of 92,000 votes. But the people of Texas were beginning to understand. The 95 counties that Yarborough carried were 74 more than he had won in 1952. Even in defeat Ralph Yarborough's stature was steadily growing as a leader and articulate spokesman for the true principles of the Democratic party.

At this point in his career, Yarborough had come to a difficult political crossroads. Twice defeated in exhausting campaigns for Governor against a well-oiled, powerful machine, he was both discouraged and in debt. His law practice had suffered because of his preoccupation with the heavy demands of political campaigning. He drew on the fundamental Henderson County training of his father and on a deep faith in the viability of our democratic institutions. Yarborough was comforted by the loyalty and dedication of Opal and his family and by his thousands of tireless campaign workers throughout the State. He also took solace from rereading Carl Sandburg's *Lincoln* and its account of Lincoln's successive defeats for the Illinois legislature, for

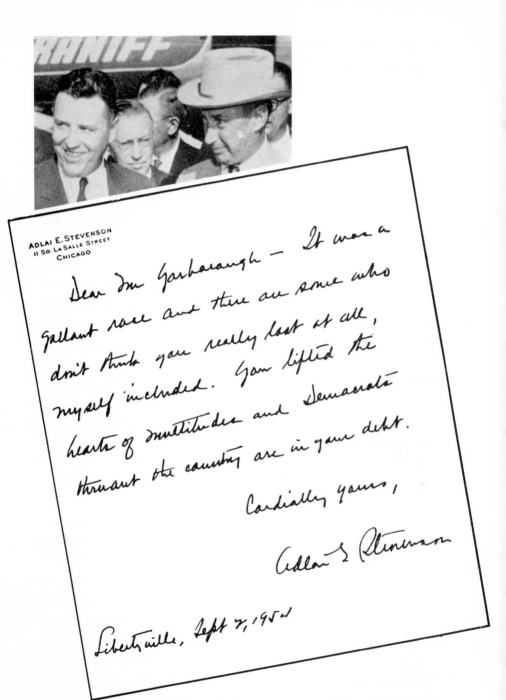

ADLAI E. STEVENSON
11 So. La Salle Street
CHICAGO

Dear Jim Yarborough — It was a gallant race and there are some who don't think you really lost at all, myself included. You lifted the hearts of multitudes and Democrats thruout the country are in your debt.

Cordially yours,

Adlai E. Stevenson

Libertyville, Sept 7, 1954

Yarborough's uphill fight against the Shivers machine in his three guberna-torial races in the 1950's attracted Nationwide admiration and interest. One of his faithful supporters was the late Adlai Stevenson, Democratic Presidential standard-bearer in 1952 and 1956. Yarborough was on hand to welcome Steven-son to Texas in October, 1955 when he arrived at the Austin Airport.

Congress, for Senator in two campaigns, and for the Vice Presidential nomination before his election as President in 1860. But when Yarborough resumed his law practice after the 1954 election, his political future appeared—to say the least—problematical, if not dismal.

Building the Party

Yarborough continued his efforts to help strengthen the loyal Democratic party in Texas. Adlai Stevenson visited Texas in 1955 and Yarborough met him at the airport. He preached ongoing organization, hard work and voter registration. He had learned of city organization needs and how to organize precincts during the 1952 and 1954 races. When 1956 came, Yarborough was undecided on whether or not to make another try for elective office. But inexorable political forces were at work. They would help shape that decision. The basis for Yarborough's charges of corruption and scandal in the State machine during the 1952 and 1954 campaigns, ignored or dismissed by Texas' institutional press, was by now making front page news.

A veterans' land scandal resulted in a prison term for State Land Commissioner Bascom Giles. An insurance expose resulted in the resignation of State Insurance Commissioner Garland Smith, a former Shivers State Campaign Chairman. John Van Cronkite, an aide to Governor Shivers, stood revealed as an "influence peddler" for a defunct insurance company.

Counted Out—1956

In the spring of 1956 Yarborough again doggedly entered the race for Governor. He again took to the campaign trail to carry his fight to the hard-pressed Shivercrats and their decaying machine. To head off a Yarborough victory the Shivercrats "drafted" their last relatively popular candidate, incumbent U.S. Senator Price Daniel. It was a bitter, hard-fought contest, enlivened by the candidacy of the colorful former Governor and Senator W. Lee "Pappy"

O'Daniel and a platform confrontation between Yarborough and extremist candidate J. Evatts Haley. O'Daniel's style and appeal to many of Yarborough's erstwhile supporters drew enough votes to force a runoff between Yarborough and Daniel.

Senator Daniel squeaked through to win the Democratic gubernatorial nomination by a margin of some 3,000 votes out of 1,390,000 votes cast, although many long-time Texas election observers were convinced that Yarborough had, in fact, won. He carried 146 of the 254 counties, up by 51 over 1954. A number of cases of election irregularities had been reported. Hundreds of marked, but uncounted, Yarborough ballots were subsequently discovered in trash heaps near polling places in several parts of the State. But under Texas law, a recount is not permitted unless alleged fraud can be proved. Unfortunately, Texas history has proved this to be a virtually impossible feat.

Counted "out" but not down, Yarborough was philosophic about his "defeat." As he had said during the campaign:

"It is a great privilege to be able to take part in these democratic campaigns. Politics is the work-a-day part of democracy and we will fight for democracy."

He urged his friends and supporters to renew their efforts in the struggle for better organization, progress, and integrity in government:

"Elections are never won by the people in the relatively short periods of formal campaigning. . . . The big money might buy an election quickly, but the people must win by day-in-day-out plugging away at the job. We must be pluggers.

"First, we must organize, organize in every precinct in the state on a seven-days-a-week, 365 days-a-year basis.

"Second, we must present the people with a program, a Democratic program.

"An organization, working all the time, and a Democratic program based on the needs and wants of the people—these are the keys to Democratic victory."

Yarborough threw his energies into the Presidential campaign for the Stevenson-Kefauver ticket as part of the loyal Democratic effort to swing Texas back into the Democratic column in 1956. But with the national sweep native son Eisenhower again carried the State, this time by a margin of 220,000 votes, or 55.3 percent.

But the winds of political change were blowing even stronger. Soon after World War II, John Gunther had described Texas in his book *Inside U.S.A.*:

"(In Texas) . . . the center of political gravity is shifting, albeit slowly, and the issue that cuts through all other issues can be expressed in one word, liberalism. . . . Ahead is . . . the education of the propertied class to social responsibility, the shift in politics caused by labor, the breakup of feudal privilege, and the development of what the state needs above all, small, home-owned, decentralized industry. Texas is tossing and stirring like a mighty giant; the picture is almost classically that of early manhood struggling with itself. It has outgrown the solid South; it is outgrowing the old colonial economy; it is becoming thoroughly weary of people like Dies and O'Daniel; it looks brightly and with stalwart hope to a better world tomorrow."

Perhaps this is what the struggle of Yarborough and the people of Texas during the 1950's was all about. Ralph Yarborough became the symbol of that "stalwart hope" for a better world in which democracy would be restored to Texas and progress of the Hogg and Allred eras would again become a reality. This time it would not be denied.

Victory and Vindication—1957

It happened suddenly. The ashes of the bitter defeat of 1956 were scarcely cold. A special election was called for the

Senate seat made vacant by the November election of Price Daniel as Governor. Dallas attorney-businessman William A. Blakley had been appointed in January in the interim. Yarborough entered for the April 2, 1957 election at the strong urging of his many loyal supporters. The same forces of reaction organized a last desperate effort to head him off. Texas law provided that in a special election the candidate winning the most votes—not necessarily a clear majority—would be the victor. The State legislature was then in session and anti-Yarborough forces attempted to change the law before the election could be held. A bill was introduced to require a run-off between the top two candidates. Such a strategy, his opponents felt, would deny Yarborough the Senate seat. But since the bill came after the cut-off date for normal consideration, 100 of the 150 House votes were required for passage. The anti-Yarborough forces fell eight votes short in their first effort to pass the bill; but a parliamentary maneuver brought the bill back to the House and it passed with 109 votes after some of the most vicious arm-twisting in Texas' legislative history.

By the time the anti-Yarborough measure reached the State Senate, a major political furor had developed. The bill was viewed by Yarborough supporters and by some impartial observers as another attempt to "steal" an election. Coming so soon after the 1956 primary race that counted Yarborough "out," it was just too much for the State Senate to swallow. Even some of the more conservative, conscientious members of the Senate refused to support this obvious attempt to block Yarborough by changing the election rules so late in the game. Moreover, many considered it a bad precedent that might come back to haunt them in future elections. The special election went on as originally scheduled.

April 2, 1957, did not begin as a Yarborough day. A heavy rain blanketed Texas and tornados were reported in many rural areas of central and north Texas. In previous elections Yarborough had run best in the rural counties and

45

good weather was conducive to a heavy Yarborough turn-out. The threat of tornados made travel to many of Texas' 9,000 polling places somewhat risky. Communications lines were out in some areas and radio broadcasts urged citizens to remain at home.

When early returns that evening showed Yarborough trailing by 75,000 votes, newsmen began calling to urge a concession statement. But Yarborough was not to be misled or denied; thousands of his loyal campaign workers labored to get every possible Yarborough voter to the polls despite the elements. Ralph Yarborough was elected to the Senate, defeating Democrat Martin Dies, Republican Thad Hutcheson and 15 others by a margin of 74,000 votes out of 875,000 cast, carrying 172 counties out of 254—up 26 over 1956.

Yarborough's faith in the democratic process and in the ultimate sound political judgment of the people of Texas was at last vindicated.

Thousands of congratulatory messages inundated newly-elected Senator Ralph Yarborough following his spectacular victory in the April 2, 1957 special election. His re-election victories for full six-year terms in 1958 and 1964 were by impressive margins.

Yarborough campaign literature from early races for Governor and Senator. Meager campaign budgets limited quantity for distribution.

Ralph Webster Yarborough took the oath of office as United States Senator from Texas on April 29, 1957. It is administered by Vice President Richard M. Nixon as Senator Lyndon B. Johnson, the Senate Majority Leader and Texas' senior Senator, looks on approvingly.

Senator Yarborough

RALPH YARBOROUGH WAS SWORN IN as United States Senator from Texas and took his seat in the Senate on April 29, 1957. He joined senior Senator Lyndon B. Johnson, the Democratic Majority Leader of the Senate, who was emerging as one of the coming leaders in the Democratic Party. In carrying out these legislative leadership duties, Johnson was greatly aided by his close personal relationship with another Texan, veteran Speaker of the House Sam Rayburn.

Yarborough's arrival in Washington indirectly helped to advance Johnson's national prominence. With the progressive Yarborough as a colleague rather than the conservative Price Daniel, Johnson's New Deal affinities revived. He left the Southern Senators' caucus, joined the Western caucus. Despite a serious heart attack, Johnson became increasingly mentioned as a leading contender for the 1960 Presidential nomination.

Both the Senate and House of Representatives in the 85th Congress were controlled by Democrats; Eisenhower had become the first President in over 100 years who failed to carry into office with him a Congress of his own party. The existing narrow Democratic margin in the Senate—48 to 47—made the new Senator from Texas extremely welcome. His election guaranteed the continuation of Democratic committee chairmen and other prerequisites of party control. The Democratic edge was now 49 to 47.

Yarborough was assigned to seats on the Interstate and Foreign Commerce Committee, the Government Operations Committee, and the Post Office and Civil Service Committee. As is characteristic of Ralph Yarborough, he plunged into his new legislative duties with enthusiasm. He studied the Senate rules to become familiar with the unique parliamentary procedures that govern debate and the daily conduct of Senate business. He attended committee meetings diligently. He studied previous legislative activities of his three committees to become more knowledgeable about the subjects within the jurisdictional areas of each. He soon gained the reputation of a Senator who did his "homework."

As the famous Texan J. Frank Dobie observed:

"I have known Ralph Yarborough as friend and man for many years. He is perhaps the best read man that Texas has ever sent to Washington. His cultivated and disciplined mind is always seeking information on subjects that government must act upon."

One of Yarborough's first successful legislative efforts was the fight for the San Angelo, Texas, multi-purpose reclamation project, which provided $32 million for the comprehensive development of the Concho River basin in west-central Texas. The bill had passed the Senate shortly before Yarborough's election, but it was stalled in the House. Soon after his arrival, Texas' junior Senator registered his strong support for the measure before the House Interior Committee while Speaker Rayburn worked to line up votes for the project in the House. It was finally reported out by the Committee. It squeezed through the House with a narrow 11-vote margin—the only reclamation project authorized by Congress that year.

When the Civil Rights bill—designed to strengthen the voting rights of all citizens—came before the Senate in July 1957, Yarborough was one of three Senators from States of the old Confederacy who voted with Majority Leader Lyndon Johnson for consideration of the bill under Senate rules. The other two were Senators Kefauver and Gore of Tennessee. It became the first civil rights bill to be enacted by Congress in 82 years.

Education Crisis

In the fall of 1957 two actions of major national importance occurred, one in the U.S., the other in the Soviet Union. Both had far-reaching implications and major impacts upon the American educational system during the 1960's.

The first was the action of President Eisenhower in calling out Federal troops to enforce a court desegregation order at Central High School in Little Rock, Arkansas. The storm of controversy in the South brought about by the 1954 Supreme Court decision outlawing racial segregation in the public school system still reflects one of our major unresolved national problems.

The second momentous 1957 event was the Soviet launching of Sputnik I into orbit. This had still more far-reaching effects upon American education, as well as spurring U.S. scientific progress and the lure of space exploration. The message of Sputnik was etched across the sky. The United States woke up to face a serious and immediate Russian challenge in the areas of basic science, applied technology and industrial know-how. We had long considered ourselves to be far ahead of the world in these fields. Despite many warnings and omens that America was lagging behind the U.S.S.R. in the training of scientists, engineers, mathemeticians and linguists, we had—like a nation of hares—napped while the plodding Soviet tortoise overtook us.

World political leaders—friend, foe and neutral alike—speculated upon how the United States would respond to this Russian challenge. They did not have to wait long. Democrats had recognized for years the need to upgrade U.S. education by federal aid. The Democrats on the Senate

Senator Yarborough logs many thousands of miles a year via plane between Washington and Texas. Despite the heavy demands of his office and the long sessions of Congress in recent years, Yarborough spends as much time as possible in his native State on speaking trips, fact-finding missions, and in meeting and talking with Texans about their views on public issues.

Labor and Public Welfare Committee saw the opportunity immediately and led in urging action. The Eisenhower Administration had to follow and support the measure, which became the National Defense Education Act of 1958. Senator Ralph Yarborough was a Senate co-sponsor of the legislation. He had transferred to the Labor and Public Welfare Committee when a vacancy occurred. Yarborough was not originally assigned to the Education Subcommittee. He started going to all its hearings, however, and Senator Hill made the assignment.

Yarborough played an active part in writing the bill in Committee. He helped steer it to passage by the Senate. He served on the joint Senate-House conference committee that resolved differences between the two versions of the measure. The National Defense Education Act was perhaps the most significant education law enacted by Congress since the Morrill Land Grant College Act of 1862. The 1958 Act marked the auspicious beginning of Yarborough's leadership role in education.

Chairman Hill of the Labor and Public Welfare Committee praised the work of freshman Senator Yarborough on the bill during Senate debate on the conference report:

"The distinguished Senator from Texas (Mr. Yarborough) has been a devoted member of the Senate Committee on Labor and Public Welfare. He made many fine contributions to the bill. He not only sat with us during the long days of hearings and executive sessions of the Committee, but he was one of the conferees on the bill. He was a most important member of the team which brings the bill to the floor of the Senate today."

Early Success

The new Senator from Texas made his influence felt in many other legislative areas as well. In 1958, Yarborough first introduced his proposals to create a Padre Island National Seashore and to extend GI Bill benefits to Cold War veterans, the two major items on his personal legislative agenda for the next few years. When the 1957-58 recession began to pinch the economy, Yarborough worked for the National Housing Act of 1958 and for the Area Redevelopment bill to assist chronically depressed sections of Texas and the Nation. He supported Massachusetts' Senator John F. Kennedy's proposal to broaden the unemployment compensation system. He also offered an amendment to an Administration tax measure to raise personal income tax exemptions from $600 to $800 per dependent, but this change was rejected. He helped pass the bill to liberalize Social Security benefits and to extend their coverage. The Senator also worked in Committee and on the Senate floor to help enact legislation to raise the salaries of postal workers. He supported a separate measure providing career incentive pay increases for members of our armed forces. Yarborough helped push the passage of the National Aeronautics and Space Act of 1958, the fountainhead of the programs for our space exploration accomplishments of the 1960's. The Manned Spacecraft Center in Houston would later play an illustrious role in America's reach toward the stars, culminating in the 1969 moon landing.

Re-Election Victory—1958

Ralph Yarborough again took to the political hustings in 1958 to seek reelection to the Senate for a full six-year term. Campaigning in the midst of pressing Senate duties is an onerous necessity for almost all incumbents. Yarborough logged many long hours in the air betwen Washington and Texas that year. Loyal, hardworking Yarborough supporters in Texas helped him with as much of the campaign burden as possible. But out on the electioneering platform, there is no substitute for the candidate himself.

Yarborough won a smashing victory in the July primary with a vote of 761,511 to 535,418 votes for his opponent, Bill Blakley, sweeping 223 counties out of 254. This was an increase of 52 counties over Yarborough's margin in 1957.

He was overwhelmingly re-elected in November by a vote of 587,030 to Republican Whittenburg's 185,926 votes, carrying a total of 249 counties. Yarborough received 74.6 percent of the vote—one of the highest percentages a Statewide candidate has ever received in Texas.

Yarborough's first, abbreviated term in the Senate had quickly won him many friends among his Senate colleagues because of his sincerity, his dedication to the principles of the Democratic party and his hard work in behalf of his State and its people.

The attitude toward the Texan among his Senate colleagues was perhaps best summed up by Minnesota's Hubert H. Humphrey:

"Ralph is an intelligent man; he is also a tireless worker and a fighter for the things in which he believes. As a consequence, he gets things done. As a member of three important Senate committees, he serves as a singularly effective representative of Texas and his fellow-Texans, as well as a valued voice and vote on all matters of critical national importance."

His dedicated efforts on the legislative committees on which he served had well prepared him to take on broader responsibilities and new opportunities in the years immediately ahead.

Up The Seniority Ladder

5

THE 1958 CONGRESSIONAL ELECTIONS that returned Ralph Yarborough to the Senate also resulted in a Democratic net gain of 13 Senate seats and 47 seats in the House of Representatives. His climb up the Senate seniority ladder was correspondingly accelerated. Yarborough, as a legislator bubbling with energy and new proposals for enactment, did not find it easy to serve the recommended silent apprenticeship. His seatmates and friends were the lively "Class of '58" Democratic Senators—Hart, Hartke, McCarthy, McGee, Muskie and Young.

On the Commerce Committee Yarborough moved up five places from the bottom of the 11-member totem pole as four freshmen Democratic Senators were added to the Committee. He moved up in rank on the Surface Transportation Subcommittee and was assigned to the Foreign Commerce Subcommittee.

Yarborough jumped three places on the Post Office and Civil Service Committee and took over chairmanship of the Civil Service Subcommittee—his first job as chairman. He also served on the Insurance Subcommittee during the 86th Congress.

The junior Senator from Texas moved up four places in seniority on the Labor and Public Welfare Committee and became chairman of the Veterans' Affairs Subcommittee. He also served on the Education and the Health Subcommittees. In all three of these fields Ralph Yarborough has made significant legislative contributions having lasting impact on the lives of many millions of Americans.

The seniority system in Congress has been the subject of academic scrutiny for many years by students of the legislative process. It has been vilified and defended, condemned as an outmoded tradition and praised as a stabilizing influence. Perhaps the best description of the attitude toward the system was given by a nine-term member of the House who observed:

"When I first came to Congress and looked at all the senior Members who were committee chairman, I concluded that the seniority system could never work. Now after 18 years here, it makes more sense to me all the time."

It is often an erratic ascent up the seniority ladder to the top rungs. Because of the quirks of political fate and the cases of abnormal longevity, there is a wide range of seemingly inconsistent behavior under the seniority system. One Senator might become chairman of a major committee after two terms or less, while another may not achieve such status until he has served three or more terms. This is because seniority is based on the length of service on a particular committee, not on the total length of service in the Senate. This general rule is subject to a number of modifications, however. A Senator does not fill more than one chairmanship of a full committee at any given time and there are cases where a top-ranking member defers to a more junior colleague because of the pressure of other Senate duties. The seniority system can be summed up in just one word—flexibility.

In 1960, during the second session of the 86th Congress, Yarborough was given another subcommittee assignment as Chairman of the Freedom of Communications Subcommittee of the Commerce Committee. This subcommittee was later to play an important role in studying the public media coverage of the Presidential campaign.

A major problem in the day-to-day operations of the sixteen regular standing legislative committees of the Senate

President John F. Kennedy presents pen to Senator Yarborough after signing Yarborough's bill creating the Padre Island National Seashore in 1962. Vice President Johnson and Congressman John Young of Corpus Christi participated in the ceremony.

is the difficulty in obtaining participation of a reasonable number of any committee's members on any given day or time. It is not unusual for a single Senator to be a member of three standing committees, twelve or fifteen subcommittees of these standing committees, plus a variety of special, select or joint committees as well.

Thus a Senator may have fire or six simultaneous committee or subcommittee meetings going on any given morning. Each of them demands his attention, his presence, his active legislative participation, and often, his vote on amendments, motions, or on entire legislative proposals during executive sessions of his committee, when bills are "marked up" or readied for approval.

An able Senator must not only have a good head and adequate legislative expertise to cope with this often chaotic system; he must also have a good sense of timing and a strong pair of legs to run from committee meeting to meeting as is sometimes required. Yarborough has been blessed with the mental and physical stamina so important to the daily life of a Senator. His wide practical experience in the law and many other fields made Yarborough particularly well-equipped to carry out the diversified duties in the Senate. As Senator Mike Mansfield of Montana expressed it:

> "Ralph Yarborough is a man of vigor, intelligence and integrity, and there is no harder worker, more diligent or conscientious member of the Senate."

Senatorial absences in this often hectic system are relieved to some extent by the informal participation of a Senator's legislative staff in committee sessions. Staff members of the subcommittees or full committees also provide information and details on legislation to individual members.

Despite the complications of the committee system and the tremendous pressure exerted on a Senator for his time and attention, it is clear that the system does work in practice. Its degree of success can be readily measured by the

Texas Democratic unity for the Kennedy-Johnson Presidential ticket in 1960 was key to election victory nationally. Senator Yarborough and the late Speaker of the House Sam Rayburn flank the candidates at arrival rally at Dallas airport.

tremendous output of legislation from each Congress and the amount of important public business conducted every day by Congressional committees.

New Duties

The exciting Presidential campaign of 1960, which returned the Democratic party to the White House, made a lasting impact on Texas, the Nation, and the world. President John F. Kennedy and Vice President Lyndon B. Johnson ushered in a new upsurge of legislative activity in which Senator Ralph Yarborough played an increasingly important part.

The election also had the effect of making Yarborough the senior Senator from Texas. A special election in Texas in May 1961 saw interim appointee William A. Blakley, a Shivers-type Democrat, defeated by Republican John G. Tower. Yarborough was also, for the first time since Reconstruction, the only Democratic Senator from the Lone Star State.

Changes in the committee makeup in 1961 moved Yarborough still higher on the Labor and Public Welfare Committee and the Post Office and Civil Service Committee. He became number four on Labor when committee colleagues Jim Murray of Montana retired and John F. Kennedy moved to 1600 Pennsylvania Avenue. He moved up to third ranking member of Post Office and maintained his same rank on the Commerce Committee. He also held his three subcommittee chairmanships—one on each standing committee.

The 87th Congress beginning in 1961 was an exceptionally busy time for Democrats. With John F. Kennedy in the White House, innovative Democratic proposals could come forward for action. It was time to work for federal aid to education, area redevelopment, medical care for the aged and other measures long delayed. The pace of Congress quickened on the "New Frontier."

Texas-made gavel is traded by Senator Yarborough for one made in Minnesota for Vice President Humphrey, presiding officer of the Senate during the Johnson Administration.

Yarborough was present when that tragic day in Dallas in November, 1963 took from America and the world the vision and leadership of President John F. Kennedy. Vice President Lyndon B. Johnson became our 36th President and the first Texan to serve in the Nation's highest office. In his address to a joint session of Congress he resolved to carry forward the programs of the Kennedy-Johnson Administration as he said "Let us continue."

In spite of the general harmony in the Texas Democratic Party in 1964 (a highly unusual and temporary situation), Senator Yarborough drew a last-minute opponent. Tied down in Washington by his legislative duties, Yarborough was reluctant to campaign until his well-financed opponent sponsored one of the most brazen slander campaigns in Texas history. After spending April touring the State and seeing the people, Yarborough was renominated in the May primary by a substantial margin, carrying 213 counties.

The 1964 campaign was the first time that President Johnson and Senator Yarborough had ever been on the ballot as Democratic running-mates. During the campaign, LBJ told the Texas voters:

". . . I don't think that Texas has had a Senator during my lifetime whose record I am more familiar with than I am with Senator Yarborough's. And I don't think Texas has had a Senator that voted for the people more than Senator Yarborough has voted for them. And no Member of the U.S. Senate has stood up and fought for me or fought for the people more since I became President than Ralph Yarborough. . . ."

Yarborough's November 1964 reelection victory over Republican George Bush for a second full term came by a margin of 330,000 votes—Yarborough's greatest numerical plurality. He carried 220 counties out of 254. The Johnson-Humphrey ticket swept to an historic landslide victory over Goldwater Republicanism and Democrats picked up 38

The Alamo, famous Texas shrine in San Antonio, was the scene of visit in September 1960 by Democratic Presidential and Vice Presidential candidates John F. Kennedy and Lyndon B. Johnson, joined by Senator Yarborough. Loyal Texas voters have kept the State in the Democratic column in the Presidential elections of 1960, 1964 and 1968.

more seats in the House. The Senate in the new 89th Congress was made up of 68 Democrats and 32 Republicans.

Appropriations Role

A major shift in committee assignments for Senator Yarborough took place when the new Congress organized. He moved from the Commerce Committee to take a seat on the powerful Appropriations Committee, the first Texan to serve on the committee in fifty years. He was assigned to the subcommittees on Agriculture, Military Construction, Legislative, Treasury-Post Office-Executive Office, and the District of Columbia Appropriations. He became the second ranking Senator on the Post Office Committee and maintained his number four spot on the Labor and Public Welfare Committee, where he also was assigned to a new subcommittee that was to become increasingly important—the Select Subcommittee on Poverty. The death of Senator McNamara of Michigan in April 1966 made Yarborough Chairman of the Labor Subcommittee.

With the organization of the 90th Congress in January 1967, Yarborough moved up to the number-three position on the Labor and Public Welfare Committee. He continued to serve as Chairman of the Labor Subcommittee. He also maintained his number two rank on the Post Office Committee, serving as Chairman of the Postal Affairs Subcommittee. His assignments on the Appropriations Committee remained the same as in the previous Congress.

Divided Government

President Johnson's decision not to seek re-election and the subsequent election of Richard Nixon to the Presidency in 1968 by a razor-thin margin over Vice President Hubert Humphrey gave the GOP control over the Executive Branch of government for the first time in eight years. It also brought major changes in the Senate and the House. Although both remained under Democratic control, Republicans gained six seats in the Senate and picked up 47 seats in

1964 Democratic ticket for President, Vice President and U.S. Senator—President Lyndon B. Johnson, Senator Hubert H. Humphrey and Senator Ralph W. Yarborough receive enthusiastic Austin airport reception. All won smashing victories at the polls as Democrats swept the Nation and padded their margins of control in the Senate and the House of Representatives.

the House of Representatives. Nixon won only slightly more than 43 per cent of the popular vote and, like Eisenhower in 1956, failed to carry into office with him a Congress of his own political party.

Following the chaotic Democratic Convention in Chicago, Ralph Yarborough had thrown his tremendous energies into the campaign for the Democratic ticket in his native Texas. He became Chairman of the Texas Citizens for Humphrey-Muskie and stumped the State for the ticket. Loyal Democrats rallied in an uphill fight and Texas remained in the Democratic column in 1968, despite some defections to Nixon and George Wallace's third party movement. Some observers attributed the feat to Yarborough's effort and appeal, since some Democratic state leaders were inactive during the campaign.

When the 91st Congress met in January, 1969, Senator Yarborough attained the top rung of the seniority ladder when he was named Chairman of the Labor and Public Welfare Committee. Chairman Lister Hill had retired at the end of the 1968 session and the second-ranking member of the Committee, Senator Wayne Morse of Oregon, had been upset in his November reelection bid.

Yarborough also became head of the Health Subcommittee and now serves on the Subcommittees on Education, Veterans Affairs', and Employment-Manpower-Poverty. In addition, he is on the Special Subcommittees on Indian Education, the Aging, and Alcoholism and Narcotics. He also chairs the Special Subcommittee on International Health, Education and Welfare Programs.

The Texan is presently the senior Democrat on the Post Office and Civil Service Committee, now chaired by Democratic Senator Gale McGee of Wyoming. (Under Senate precedent, a Senator can chair only one full committee at a time.) Yarborough maintains an energetic role in postal and civil service matters. He also serves on the Senate's Special Committee on Aging and the Select Committee on Nutrition and Human Needs.

Chairman Yarborough consults with Senate Majority Leader Mike Mansfield of Montana on details of legislative scheduling of important measure favorably reported by Yarborough's Labor and Public Welfare Committee.

1964 Executive session of the Senate Labor and Public Welfare Committee considers pending legislation. Senator Yarborough (left) listens as veteran Chairman Lister Hill of Alabama explains amendment. Others, from left to right, are Mr. John Forsythe (General Counsel of the Committee), Senators Harrison A. Williams, Jr., of New Jersey, and Senator Claiborne Pell of Rhode Island.

Texas' senior Senator has retained his influential seat on the vitally important Appropriations Committee. He is Chairman of the Subcommittee on Treasury—Post Office—Executive Office, which has budgetary jurisdiction over these two Departments and the White House, Bureau of the Budget and related appropriations business. He also serves on the Subcommittees on Agriculture and related agricultural agencies, Military Construction, Legislative, and the District of Columbia.

The role of the Appropriations Committee in the Senate can be summed up in one word: power. Years of effort to enact a law to provide Federal funds to build a flood control dam, for example, will mean next to nothing if funds are not then appropriated for the actual construction. The original law would merely authorize the dam-building. A subsequent action is required by the Appropriations Committee—usually acting on recommendation of its responsible subcommittee—to vote the funds to do the job.

Obviously, a Senator who works to pass a bill authorizing a particular program is in a key position to help obtain the necessary funds to implement it if he also serves on the Appropriations Committee. Thus, in such fields as education, health, veterans, agriculture, conservation, and the Texan's many other areas of concern to Texas and the Nation, Senator Yarborough's efforts are greatly strengthened by his high-leverage position on the powerful Appropriations Committee.

Having reached the top of the seniority ladder as Chairman of the Senate Labor and Public Welfare Committee, Senator Ralph Yarborough can be counted on to exercise his great power effectively and judiciously. He brings vital new leadership ability to help meet the Nation's urgent human needs looming so importantly for our citizens in the years ahead.

6
Mr. Chairman

JANUARY 1969 FOUND Texas Senator Ralph Yarborough in an historic dilemma. He was the top surviving Democrat on two important Committees—Labor and Public Welfare as well as Post Office and Civil Service. Since Democrats controlled the 91st Congress, he was in line for not just one—but two—full committee chairmanships. However, he could, under Senate precedent, retain only one.

With the retirement of veteran Alabama Chairman Lister Hill, the number two Democrat—Morse of Oregon would normally have moved up to the chairmanship of Labor and Public Welfare. But, after 24 years in the Senate, Morse was defeated for re-election in a major political upset. Senator Mike Monroney, the Oklahoma Democrat who headed the Post Office Committee, had likewise been beaten in another upset after serving 30 years in Congress—six terms in the House and three terms in the Senate.

Momentous Decision

The Texan was torn by conscience, duty and inclination in making his choice of a chairmanship. His record of service on both committees had been long and illustrious. His legislative leadership capabilities were highly in demand. Never one to agonize in indecision, Yarborough chose the chairmanship of the Labor and Public Welfare Committee. He is the first Texan to become chairman of a regular standing Senate Committee since the 1953 retirement of the late Tom Connally, then Chairman of the Foreign Relations Committee.

Senator Yarborough's lifelong interest in education and health and his overriding concern for the common man were the deciding factors in his choice. The Labor and Public Welfare Committee has legislative jurisdiction over programs that touch the lives of every American citizen. As former President Johnson once told Yarborough:

"Ralph, your Committee was responsible for eighty percent of the legislation enacted by the historic 89th Congress."

The Labor and Public Welfare Committee cuts one of the broadest swaths of legislative authority in the Senate. It has jurisdiction over vastly important areas of human endeavor such as the purviews of the Department of Health, Education and Welfare, including the Office of Education; the Public Health Service; the National Institutes of Health and the Food and Drug Administration. The Committee is also the legislative overseer of the Department of Labor, the Veterans' Administration, the National Labor Relations Board, the Office of Economic Opportunity, the Railroad Retirement Board and many other agencies and bureaus whose programs affect the well-being of every American.

Senate Labor and Public Welfare Committee Chairman Yarborough is shown with his veteran predecessor, Senator Lister Hill of Alabama. Hill served as Chairman of the Committee for 14 years before his retirement from the Senate in 1968.

Yarborough confers with another famous Texan, the late Senator Tom Connally. Connally was Chairman of the Senate Foreign Relations Committee until he retired in 1953, after serving for four consecutive terms.

Famous Committee Leaders

The Labor and Public Welfare Committee has been one of the prime breeding grounds for national political leaders. During the past 20 years, two Presidents-to-be served on the Committee—John F. Kennedy and Richard M. Nixon. A number of leading Presidential candidates and aspirants have also sat on the Committee—Senators Barry Goldwater, Hubert H. Humphrey, Strom Thurmond, Robert A. Taft and Robert F. Kennedy. The present Democratic Whip, Edward M. Kennedy, is a member of Chairman Yarborough's Committee.

Many distinguished Senators of both parties have served terms as Chairman of the Labor and Public Welfare Committee. Since World War II, these chairmen have been:

80th Congress	—Senator Robert A. Taft (R., Ohio)
81st	—Senator Elbert D. Thomas (D., Utah)
82nd	—Senator James E. Murray (D., Mont.)
83rd	—Senator H. Alexander Smith (R., N.J.)
84th—90th	—Senator Lister Hill (D., Ala.)
91st—	—Senator Ralph W. Yarborough (D., Tex.)

In the 91st Congress the Committee is composed of 17 Senators—10 Democrats and 7 Republicans. The party ratio on each Senate committee reflects, as nearly as possible, the proportionate party makeup of the Senate as a whole. There are six freshman Senators on the Committee—3 Democrats and 3 Republicans. These Senators serve on the Labor and Public Welfare Committee in the 91st Congress, ranked in order of their Committee seniority:

Democrats

Ralph W. Yarborough, Texas (Chrmn.)
Jennings Randolph, West Virginia
Harrison A. Williams, New Jersey
Claiborne Pell, Rhode Island
Edward M. Kennedy, Massachusetts
Gaylord Nelson, Wisconsin
Walter F. Mondale, Minnesota
Thomas F. Eagleton, Missouri
Alan Cranston, California
Harold E. Hughes, Iowa

Republicans

Jacob Javits, New York
Winston L. Prouty, Vermont
Peter H. Dominick, Colorado
George Murphy, California
Richard S. Schweiker, Pennsylvania
William B. Saxbe, Ohio
Ralph T. Smith, Illinois

The Legislative Reorganization Act of 1946, which sets forth the jurisdictions of various Congressional committees, describes the current purview of the Senate Labor and Public Welfare Committee:

> *"(1) Measures relating to education, labor, or public welfare generally, (2) Mediation and arbitration of labor disputes, (3) Wages and hours of labor, (4) Convict labor and the entry of goods made by convicts into interstate commerce, (5) Regulation or prevention of importation of foreign laborers under contract (6) Child labor, (7) Labor statistics, (8) Labor standards, (9) School-lunch program, (10) Vocational rehabilitation, (11) Railroad labor and railroad retirement and unemployment, (12) United States Employees' Compensation Commission, (13) Columbia Institution for the Deaf, Dumb, and Blind; Howard University; Freedmen's Hospital; and St. Elizabeth's Hospital (in the District of Columbia), (14) Public health and quarantine, (15) Welfare of miners, (16) Vocational rehabili-*

tation and education of veterans, (17) Veterans' hospitals, medical care and treatment of veterans, (18) Soldiers' and sailors' civil relief, (19) Readjustment of servicemen to civil life."..

The Committee's offices occupy Suite 4230 of the New Senate Office Building. The main hearing room for the Committee adjoins the administrative offices of Committee staff employees. The Committee staff is made up of highly specialized attorneys, researchers and other experts with far-ranging experience in the sweeping jurisdictional areas of the Committee. In addition, of course, the staff includes a number of clerical and secretarial employees. Part of the staff serves the needs of the Chairman, the various Subcommittee Chairmen and other majority members of the Committee. Other qualified staff specialists and clerical employees report to the minority members of the Committee.

Like most standing committees of the Senate, Chairman Yarborough's Committee has regularly established meeting days—the second and fourth Thursdays of each month while the Senate is in session. These days may be used for hearings by the full Committee or for executive sessions to consider bills reported favorably by various subcommittees. An agenda is provided in advance so that Committee members may be prepared to discuss the legislative matters to be presented by Chairman Yarborough.

To facilitate the consideration and movement of legislation referred to the Committee, Yarborough has set up seven regular subcommittees and a number of special subcommittees. The following Senators serve as regular Subcommittee Chairmen in the 91st Congress:

Health—Yarborough of Texas
Education—Pell of Rhode Island
Labor—Williams of New Jersey
Employment-Manpower-Poverty—Kennedy of Massachusetts
Veterans Affairs—Cranston of California
Railroad Retirement—Eagleton of Missouri
Migratory Labor—Mondale of Minnesota

Late into most evenings, Senator Yarborough works with key staff aides on mountain of correspondence, constituent casework, speeches for the next busy day. Yarborough has earned the reputation as one of the Senate's most conscientious and hard-working members.

Each of these Chairmen is serving in his abovesaid capacity for the first time. Special subcommittees under Yarborough include those on the Aging, Indian Education, Alcoholism and Narcotics, Arts and Humanities, International Health, Education and Labor Programs, National Science Foundation, and Evaluation and Planning of Social Programs. The work of the various regular and special subcommittees is coordinated under the supervision of the Chairman.

Committee at Work

Chairman Yarborough's Committee is one of the busiest in the Senate. During the 90th Congress under Chairman Hill, some 433 bills and resolutions were referred to the Committee; the Committee or its subcommittees held hearings on 87 of these measures. Forty of them were reported to the Senate and subsequently enacted into law—a very high "batting average" for any Senate Committee's effort.

The Committee's activities also included hearings or investigations on other important subjects. They covered such diverse matters as Indian problems, an examination of the "war on poverty," scientific manpower utilization, equal employment opportunity, railroad retirement, manpower implications of the Selective Service Act, labor union welfare and pension funds, and the problems of the aged.

No two Congressional committees function in quite the same way. The factors that make them all different are intricate. A committee's character is determined in part by its legislative jurisdiction; the political motivations, objectives and personalities of the chairman and other members of the committee; the weight of the committee's workload; the quantity and quality of its staff and a hundred more subtle traits.

One very significant factor affecting committee operation in the 91st Congress is the cleavage of the massive force of the Federal government, politically divided between a Republican Executive branch and a Democratically-controlled Legislative branch. Thus, the joint responsibility for initiating and enacting a legislative program, normally shared by the Executive and the Congress, is lacking. This unusual situation places an abnormally heavy responsibility on the Democratic party leadership of the Senate and House, and a corresponding burden on the committee chairmen, who are an essential part of that legislative leadership.

Conversely, the Republican Executive must be judicious in proposing legislation within certain limitations, in recognition of the opposition party's control of Congress. Legislative-Executive relationships can be touchy in such a situation. Early in the Nixon Administration, an attempt was made to close the narcotics treatment facility in Fort Worth. Yarborough's strong fight to maintain this needed hospital facility finally convinced Health, Education and Welfare Secretary Finch that it should remain in operation.

Chairman Yarborough

Not all 91st Congress committee chairmen, however, see their responsibilities in this situation in a similar light. Some, such as Chairman Ralph Yarborough, strongly believe that the role of a committee is not merely to examine and react to the legislative proposals that are initiated by the Republican President. Yarborough, for example, actively advocates legislation that he feels is needed to meet critical needs in health, education and other fields. Soon after becoming Chairman, Yarborough said:

"I did not accept the Chairmanship of the Senate Labor and Public Welfare Committee to liquidate programs."

Other less dynamic chairmen often choose to avoid a legislative leadership role during a period of divided government. They tend to emphasize the oversight function of their committees, stressing their continuous evaluation of the Executive's administration of Federal programs within the committee's jurisdiction. Some may act merely to extend existing programs.

Senate committees have the duty of considering Executive appointments—ranging from Supreme Court Justices to Ambassadors, from Cabinet members to the heads of regulatory agencies—depending on the purview of the various committees. For example, Chairman Yarborough's Committee considered the Cabinet appointment of Secretary of Labor George P. Shultz when he was nominated by President Nixon in January 1969. The Committee also held hearings on many other subcabinet and agency officials whose appointments required Senate confirmation. Such Presidential nominations are usually approved by the committees after routine hearings and are forwarded to the Senate for equally routine confirmation. Exceptions to the routine make headlines, such as when the Senate refused to confirm President Eisenhower's nomination of Atomic Energy Commission Chairman Lewis Strauss as Secretary of Commerce during the 1950's.

Powers and Duties

The range of powers of any committee chairman are both little known and awesome in their scope:

- He may determine the organizational structure of the committee, the designation of various subcommittees, their jurisdiction and who shall be their chairmen.
- He decides the major direction and emphasis of the committee's activities by setting the priorities for hearings on bills before the committee and how long such hearings shall continue. He even determines the order in which bills shall be considered for further committee action when hearings are completed.
- He presides over meetings of his committee, exercising his powers in recognizing other members, in considering amendments to bills, in proposing alternative language to the legislation being discussed and in determining the way in which bills reported fa-

vorably by his committee shall be presented on the floor of the Senate. He may also call special meetings to consider priority measures.

- He has wide latitude in the hiring and supervision of committee staff personnel.
- He can direct special committee studies of legislative or administrative subjects within its scope and can approve travel for special field hearings.
- His position alone usually commands special attention for matters he addresses to an Executive agency over which his committee has legislative jurisdiction.

The effectiveness of any committee chairman depends, to a large extent, on how wisely he exercises his vast powers in his dealings with committee colleagues of both parties. Chairman Ralph Yarborough's sympathetic understanding of people was augmented by his judicial experience on the bench in Texas. He early developed attributes of mind and character that contribute to his success in carrying out his new responsibilities. He is firm in his own philosophic and political beliefs, but respects the viewpoints of those who may differ with him. Impatient to convert words to deeds, Yarborough has sometimes been known to ruffle the feathers of colleagues who did not share his enthusiasm for getting the job done. But he listens and can be convinced, on occasion, by political friend and foe. He is fair in presiding over his committee, allocating ample time to opposition members in the questioning of witnesses or in offering amendments.

Texas' beloved writer, the late J. Frank Dobie, said of Yarborough:

"Like other individuals, he travels in a certain direction, but his mind is not closed to facts and conditions warranting a change of mind. The power of his intellect to weigh knowledge and to judge justly is his."

His good friend Senator Lister Hill of Alabama, the former Committee Chairman made this observation:

"Ralph Yarborough brings his enthusiasm and vitality to every phase of the legislative process. He is patient

Senator Yarborough explains provisions of Cold War GI program of educational and training benefits to group of young Navy enlisted men. Yarborough authored the important law, finally enacted in 1966 after an eight year legislative struggle.

Senator Yarborough's busy schedule includes meetings with Texas visitors on dozens of important subjects. Here he reports on public works project progress to delegations of the Trinity Improvement Association and the Cameron County Water Control and Improvement District No. 5.

and judicious as Chairman at public hearings, a wise counselor in executive sessions, a forceful speaker on the Floor of the Senate, and at all times a vigorous advocate of the interests of Texas and her people."

In addition to his leadership role within the committee, Chairman Yarborough customarily manages on the Senate floor the major bills that are reported favorably by his Committee. If he chooses, he may delegate a part of this responsibility to one of the Subcommittee Chairmen who may have special expertise or a personal political stake in a particular bill.

Senate Office

A competent and dedicated office staff is a mainstay of prime importance to every Senator. This is particularly so in the case of a committee chairman, whose workload is many times heavier than that of other Senators. Each Senator is allocated funds to hire competent professional staff personnel and clerical employees to help run his office. These people help answer constituent mail, handle a variety of constituent requests, schedule appointments, help resolve problems with government agencies and take on dozens of other such duties.

The amount of office funds allowed a Senator is based on the "population class" of his State. Senators from very populous States such as Texas, New York, California and Pennsylvania are provided greater office expense allowances than are Senators from sparsely populated States such as Nevada, Wyoming or Alaska.

As in the case of most Senators, Yarborough's principal aides consist of an Administrative Assistant, a Legislative Assistant, a Press Secretary and a personal secretary. These posts are all filled by Texans. Each of these aides brings a high level of experience, professional skill and integrity to the position he holds. Others on Senator Yarborough's staff are specialists in research, in constituent "casework," which involves dealings with Executive agencies, and experts in legislative fields of importance to the State. A number of typists, file clerks, and other clerical personnel round out the competent Yarborough staff "team." Staffers in Yarborough's office in Austin toil throughout the year to assist and advise Texans on thousands of problems involving the Federal government.

Texas Delegation

One invariable hallmark of an effective committee chairman such as Senator Ralph Yarborough is his close working relationship with his party colleagues in the House of Representatives. Texas has one of the largest delegations in the House. In the 91st Congress it had 23 Congressmen— 20 Democrats and 3 Republicans. The powerful Texas contingent has four House Committee Chairmen—more than any other State. W. R. (Bob) Poage of Waco chairs the Agriculture Committee. George H. Mahon of Lubbock presides over Appropriations. Wright Patman of Texarkana is Chairman of the Banking and Currency Committee. Olin (Tiger) Teague of College Station leads the Veterans Affairs' Committee.

Texas' problems of mutual interest are discussed frequently by Senator Yarborough at luncheon meetings with the Texas Democratic House delegation. Individualistic men with strong and varying views on public policy, the Texas Democrats work together on projects of particular interest to Texas communities. Senator Yarborough can keep a friendly eye on the Congressmen's local bills when they are under consideration by the Senate.

When Senator Yarborough embarked on his challenging new assignment as Chairman of the Labor and Public Welfare Committee, his new responsibilities and his enlarged powers assumed far-reaching importance to the State of Texas and its 11 million citizens. Indeed, the broad sweep of the programs coming before his Committee makes a powerful impact on the daily lives of all U.S. citizens. It is difficult to measure this impact, however, in terms of individual lives. It can mean a better educational opportunity for some, the likelihood of a healthier, longer life for others, a better, higher paid job, a regular railroad retirement or veterans' pension check, employment training, or the countless other boons that may come to citizens through enlightened governmental policies.

Texas' Billions

One measure of the scope of Yarborough's Labor and Public Welfare Committee is the amount of Federal dollars going into Texas alone during the fiscal year ending June 30, 1968. Flowing from programs solely within his jurisdictional area as Chairman, Texas' share of these Federal programs was:

Department of Health, Education and Welfare	$1,751,766,595
Veterans Administration	672,830,570
Department of Labor	78,577,450
Railroad Retirement Board	67,343,309
Office of Economic Opportunity	64,213,699
National Science Foundation	13,731,082
National Labor Relations Board	1,279,339
Federal Mediation & Conciliation Service	169,107
National Foundation on Arts & Humanities	167,973
National Mediation Board	17,022
Total-Fiscal Year 1968	$2,650,096,146

This one-year Texas total from programs within Chairman Yarborough's Labor and Public Welfare Committee jurisdiction is more than the entire Federal budget only 50 years ago!

On a national basis, the total amount allocated to all states for these federal programs emanating from Yarborough's committee was almost 60 billion dollars for the same fiscal year—about one-third of the total federal budget expenditures.

As Texas' sole voice on the Senate Appropriations Committee, Senator Yarborough has, of course, a staggering responsibility in helping to allocate almost $200 billion in Federal funds as part of the Committee's annual budget consideration process. For the fiscal year ending June 30, 1968, more than $12 billion was spent in Texas for all Federal programs. About $6.4 billion of this total was spent upon Department of Defense and space program activities. The Agriculture Appropriations Subcommittee, of which Yarborough is a member, allocated to Texas another $1 billion for various farm programs. Yarborough is also Chairman of the Treasury—Post Office—Executive Office Subcommittee. As such, he helped handle over $600 million of Texas' Federal fund allocations in the postal and monetary areas. Programs of the Department of Transportation and the Department of Housing and Urban Development totaled another $1 billion in Texas alone. The Senator sat in consideration of these allocations also.

Senator Ralph Yarborough could well merit the prized title of "Mr. Chairman" for his diligent legislative labors over the past 12 years. His high position is due to the workings of the seniority system, but the effectiveness with which he uses the position for the benefit of Texas and the Nation is due to his personal dedication, intelligence and effort. Few others have already contributed so much to the well-being of the people of Texas and our Nation.

Sheet of Speaker Sam Rayburn commemorative stamps is purchased by Senator Yarborough, a member of the Senate Post Office & Civil Service Committee, from J. Edward Day, Postmaster General in the Kennedy Administration.

Yarborough and Education

7

EVER SINCE HIS EARLY EXPERIENCES as a teen-age school teacher in Henderson and as a law school instructor at the University of Texas, Ralph Yarborough has maintained an active interest in matters affecting education. His subsequent legal work after World War II in behalf of the Texas State Teachers' Association gave him additional insight into the problems of our educational system.

Like many other Senators on the Labor and Public Welfare Committee, which has Federal legislative responsibility in the field of education, Yarborough was concerned about the future of the American school system. "It has been my policy," he said in 1964, "to view education needs as a continuing national emergency." Many complex questions were and still are involved. What should be the proper Federal role in assisting the States and local school districts to provide the level of quality education for our young people in our rapidly changing world? Would the allocation of Federal dollars disorient or even usurp control of the administration of our long-established local school systems? What are the dimensions of financial need for new schools, new courses, new technology, and better pay for our teachers? What should be done to attract and to better train teachers to solve the existing shortages?

These and similar questions were not new. White House Conferences of our Nation's educational leaders had weighed such problems during the 1950's. Sputnik I gave new urgency to the need for prompt solutions. The reluctance of the Eisenhower Administration to acknowledge education as a national problem was to make it a national issue in the 1960 Presidential campaign.

Many forces were at work to compel decisive action. The postwar "baby crop" was causing serious overcrowding of existing school facilities in many areas. Local property taxes to finance education were reaching exorbitant levels. Teachers' salaries, already scandously low, were not nearly keeping pace with rising living costs; thus the profession was not attracting nearly enough qualified young teachers even to replace those leaving for greener fields or retiring each year. The challenge of Russian technology dictated a corresponding response, a raising of educational standards in our modern industrial society, compelling heavier demands on our educational system. The Supreme Court's desegregation decision in 1954 added yet another thorny political and social dimension to the already complex problem.

Losing Battles

As early as 1949, the Senate had passed a Federal aid to education bill proposed by President Harry S. Truman and supported by the late Republican Senator Robert A. Taft of Ohio. But the bill was killed by the House Education and Labor Committee after it became bogged down in the "church-state" controversy, an issue as old as the Republic itself. No Federal funds had ever been made available to a school system run under religious auspices, in keeping with the principle of the separation of church and state that is implicit in the First Amendment to the U.S. Constitution. Later, several abortive efforts were made during the Eisenhower years to enact Federal education assistance to the

States to upgrade school facilities and teachers' salary levels. In 1957, such an education bill was narrowly rejected in the House by a five-vote margin.

Senator Yarborough was convinced that both long and short range educational needs could be met only by joint Federal, State, and local cooperation. He staunchly opposed any Federal controls over local school systems. Early in 1959, Yarborough co-sponsored legislation authorizing Federal grants for school construction and/or teachers' salaries. In the Education Subcommittee on which he served, he worked diligently to help shape a sound education proposal just as he had done earlier in the enactment of the National Defense Education Act. Committee Chairman Lister Hill of Alabama, a long-time advocate of education legislation, reported the bill in behalf of the majority in September, 1959. It was subsequently debated, amended and passed by the Senate in February, 1960 by a 51 to 34 roll-call vote.

After a bitter floor battle, a separate version of the education bill was passed by the House of Representatives in May—the first time in history that the House had ever approved a general Federal education aid bill. However, the solid opposition of Republicans on the House Rules Committee blocked the education measure from going to a Senate-House conference for resolution of the differences between the two versions. The bill died, but progress had been made.

In 1961 the new Kennedy Administration reopened the legislative drive for Federal aid to education. Senator Yarborough was once more in the thick of the fight as a co-sponsor of the General School Aid bill. Under the leadership of Education Subcommittee Chairman Wayne Morse, the $2.5 billion measure was approved by the Labor and Public Welfare Committee and was passed by the Senate in May. But a companion measure in the House suffered the same old fate; it was again stymied in the House Rules Committee.

Senators Lee Metcalf of Montana (left) and Jennings Randolph of West Virginia confer with Senator Yarborough prior to meeting of his subcommittee to consider Yarborough's Cold War GI bill, subsequently enacted into law by Congress.

The 88th Congress, however, achieved a degree of success in the education field in other areas. Yarborough of Texas was again in the vanguard of action as the co-sponsor of the Higher Education Facilities Act of 1963. The new law, as signed by President Kennedy, authorized $1.2 billion in Federal grants for the construction or improvement of both public and private higher education facilities. Yarborough also co-sponsored the Health Professions Educational Assistance Act of 1963. It provided Federal funds for construction and renovation of medical and dental schools and for loans to students attending such schools. Yarborough co-sponsored, and the Congress extended, the National Defense Education Act and the programs giving Federal school construction and maintenance assistance to so-called "impacted" school districts affected by Federal installations. These were districts whose existing school facilities were strained or overwhelmed by the enrollment of children of Federal employees, both military and civilian. Texas was one of the major beneficiaries of this important program, with more than 250 school districts receiving Federal funds.

Libraries for People

Ralph Yarborough has long been a lover of books. His work as a student in the library at Sam Houston State College and the University of Texas law library deepened his affection for our cultural heritage. It was only natural that he would sponsor legislation in the Senate to provide Federal support for our Nation's libraries. Beginning in the Eisenhower years, Yarborough worked with college libraries in their efforts to enact a federal program for support of the libraries in institutions of higher education. He was the Senate sponsor of a bill recognizing the importance of library needs; not all aid should go to classroom construction alone, he thought. This program was ultimately incorporated in the Higher Education Assistance Act.

In 1960 he helped enact the Library Services Act, extending the original 1956 law for five years. Four years later, he likewise helped to enact legislation that extended the Act to cities as well as rural areas and provided Federal matching funds for construction of public library buildings and for operations of libraries. In recognition of his legislative achievements, Yarborough was named an honorary member of the Texas Library Association in 1969—the only honorary membership it ever bestowed.

Education Milestones—1965

The election of President Johnson in 1964, coupled with the overwhelming Democratic majorities in the Senate and House of Representatives in the 89th Congress, made possible the enactment of far-reaching education legislation. The Elementary and Secondary Education Act of 1965, co-sponsored by Senator Yarborough and steered through his Committee to passage, was a landmark achievement. Yarborough described the educational need in these terms:

> "We are trying to avoid a crisis through education and job opportunities—a crisis that would be caused by unleashing legions of untrained, undisciplined, uncontrolled, unemployed young people in the streets of America."

The first general Federal education aid bill ever enacted by Congress was the culmination of the many years of concentrated effort by Senate and House advocates, allied with educational and public interest groups throughout the country.

The new law provided Federal grants of some $1.3 billion annually to States and school districts to help finance a wide range of programs—funds for textbooks and library resources, special programs for children in low-income neighborhoods, supplementary education centers, regional educational research and training facilities. Also included were new programs to educate the deaf and blind and to aid

Senator Yarborough is joined by Vice President Humphrey and Congressman Eligio (Kika) de la Garza at October, 1968 dedication of the new $15 million bilingual Vocational Technical Center in Harlingen, Texas. Yarborough pioneered the bilingual education program and has been a leader in improving vocational training programs.

Senator Yarborough takes a deep interest in young people and their ambitions. Here, he hosts a group of University of Texas students in his office before accompanying them to the gallery to observe a session of the Senate.

children of limited English-speaking ability. Provision was made for assistance to rural schools in preparing project applications and funds were earmarked to strengthen State education departments. As a result, almost 90 per cent of America's 53 million school children have benefited from the Act.

The senior Senator from Texas sponsored an allocation formula amendment, included in the Act, to provide the equitable distribution of funds. The formula was based on the number of low-income families in each State and on the State's average expenditure per school child. During the first year of the new education law, Texas received some $113.5 million in Federal grant assistance.

The Higher Education Act of 1965, also co-sponsored by Yarborough, provided new programs to assist qualified high school graduates to attend college. They included scholarships, graduate fellowships, low-interest loans to students and a work-study program. The new law also provided assistance to colleges to improve their academic standards, expansion of college libraries and establishment of a National Teachers Corps. Yarborough's special interest was in providing Federal grants to students for scholarships. He pointed out that loan programs alone would not enable the low-income gifted student to go to college. He urged strenuously the inclusion of scholarships in the National Defense Education Act in 1958, but when that battle was lost, he continued the fight. Yarborough was among those who would not let the idea be dropped, and eventually the program was enacted.

During these historic "breakthrough" years, virtually every piece of education legislation was marked by the RWY brand of the Senator from Texas. Yarborough was involved at every twist and turn of threading the complex parliamentary labyrinth—the drafting and sponsorship efforts, the tedious hearings and markup sessions of his subcommittee and the full committee, the amending process to improve the bill. Yarborough battled constantly in the frequently dif-

President Johnson presents congratulations and ceremonial pen to Senator Ralph Yarborough on the approval of fund legislation for the National Teachers Corps in May, 1966. Yarborough was a major Senate backer of the proposal.

ficult Senate floor fights, working to defeat crippling amendments offered by opponents or in proposing amendments of his own to strengthen and improve legislation. At the end of the maze, he was invariably one of the Senate conferees appointed to meet with their House counterparts to resolve differences between versions of a bill. Yarborough's Texas "horse trading" ability was a valuable asset in such conference bargaining sessions.

More Legislative Gains

The list of education measures enacted over the years in which Ralph Yarborough played a key role reads like a modern history of the Congress in this crucial field. They cover the broad range of education-related laws such as the College Housing program, the Vocational Education Act, the Educational Television program, the National Science Foundation, the College Classroom Construction program, Adult Basic Education, Headstart, Job Corps, VISTA and other anti-poverty programs. The RWY brand is on them all.

The Texan's skilled legislative touch was also evident in the creation of the Peace Corps, the Manpower Development and Training Act, the Student Exchange program, School Lunch and School Milk programs, the Nurses' Training Act, formula grants to graduate Public Health Schools and the Indian Education program. Yarborough helped enact the Community Mental Health Act, Comprehensive Health Planning Act, the Community Health Facilities and Services Act, special education programs for the deaf, blind, and disabled, and many other wide-ranging educational programs.

Bilingual Education

A uniquely successful education program, sponsored and steered to enactment by Senator Yarborough in 1967, is the Bilingual Education program. The legislation grew out of several education conferences in the Southwest that fo-

Yarborough examines 24 foot letter of appreciation presented by Armando Rodriguez following enactment by Congress of his bilingual education bill.

cused attention on the language learning barrier affecting over 1.7 million children of Spanish-speaking families in Texas, New Mexico, Arizona, Colorado and Southern California.

Yarborough had attended such meetings and had studied the problem, which he readily understood from his years in El Paso. He knew that the road out of poverty must begin with the young. He reaffirmed his faith in education as the key to increased earning capacity and a better life. But the English language barrier confronting many of these children from Spanish-speaking families, when added to their economic and cultural disadvantages, presented severe, often insurmountable, handicaps in their early school years.

The Yarborough Bilingual Education bill enacted by Congress is helping to solve this problem. It provides Federal funds to school districts for bilingual education programs. Priority goes to those districts with the largest numbers of children from such non-English-speaking backgrounds. The law also provides funds for graduate fellowships for teacher training in the bilingual field.

Veterans' Rights

Perhaps Ralph Yarborough will be best known in future generations for his relentless fight to enact the "Cold War" GI Bill of Rights for veterans serving after the January 31, 1955 cut-off date for benefits under the Korean War GI Bill.

The years-long struggle began in 1958 when Yarborough introduced his original Cold War GI Bill. Despite the opposition of the Eisenhower Administration, he steered it through both his Veterans' Affairs Subcommittee and the Labor and Public Welfare Committee. It passed the Senate by a vote of 57 to 31 in July 1959, only to die in the House Veterans' Affairs Committee. But the fight had only begun; the Senator does not suffer defeat easily.

DALLAS MORNING NEWS   Thursday, July 22, 1965

CAMPAIGNER

WITH BEST WISHES TO SENATOR
RALPH YARBOROUGH

Yarborough reintroduced the measure in 1961 and again it was favorably reported to the Senate despite the opposition of the Kennedy Administration. The long-stalled bill was finally debated in the Senate late in the 1962 session, but Congress adjourned without taking final action. Again in 1963 Yarborough introduced the Cold War GI measure and again it failed.

The persistent Texan refused to quit the fight. He was convinced that returning veterans from Vietnam and other American military outposts around the world were entitled to readjustment and educational benefits as much as the veterans of World War II and Korea. During his visits to our military and naval installations in far-off parts of the globe, Yarborough had talked with American servicemen. He believed that—despite bureaucratic opposition—a full-scale program was needed to assist these young Americans in their readjustment period after returning home. He knew also that the public investment made in training, education, and other GI benefits after World War II and Korea had paid dividends to our Nation many times over.

When the 89th Congress convened in January 1965, Yarborough again introduced the bill—for the fourth time—and it was passed by the Senate in July, 1965—this time by a vote of 69 to 17. Major veterans' organizations rallied behind the measure. It was favorably reported by the House Veterans' Affairs Committee, amended, and passed by the lately enlightened House in February 1966.

The Cold War GI Bill was signed into law by President Johnson in a special ceremony on March 3, 1966. In his remarks, President Johnson jocularly referred to the efforts of Senator Yarborough and House Veterans' Affairs Chairman Teague:

"I just had my budget busted wide open this morning by my colleagues from Texas, but it was on behalf of soldiers who needed education. If it were going to be busted, it couldn't be busted for a better purpose."

Yarborough's tenacity had made it possible for an estimated 7 million American veterans, including more than 400,000 Texans, to become the bill's grateful beneficiaries. Eligibility is based on service in our Armed Forces since January 31, 1955, for at least a 180-day period. The broad-gauged law provides for college scholarships and other educational and training benefits, home and farm loan guarantees, Federal job preference, job counseling, job placement and other benefits. The pen that Senator Yarborough received from the President at the bill signing ceremony was perhaps the trophy that he had worked hardest to obtain in all his Senate years. In 1967 Yarborough succeeded in adding amendments to the law to increase monthly benefits for veterans and dependents and to broaden the training programs to include on-the-farm and on-the-job training and flight training eligibility.

Joint Senate-House conference committee meets to resolve differences between versions of public health bill. Former Chairman Hill presides in this 88th Congress meeting. Senator Yarborough is now Chairman of the Health Subcommittee, as well as the full Committee.

Senator Yarborough, working late into the night in a deserted corridor of the Senate Office Building, confers with Administrative Assistant Gene Godley on the next morning's legislative schedule.

New Frontiers in Education

The senior Senator from Texas is already looking ahead at new educational needs in the decade of the 1970's. He is contemplating the role he can play as Chairman of the Labor and Public Welfare Committee in helping to meet our growing national requirements. In the 91st Congress that convened in January 1969, Yarborough introduced two far-reaching new education bills. The Educational Technology Act of 1969 provides for the training of teachers in the use of the newest technological facilities available in education. It also gives financial assistance to schools and colleges in the acquisition of the needed equipment. Yarborough's Children with Learning Disabilities Act of 1969 authorizes the development of more adequate educational opportunities for the more than one million children whose handicapped conditions require special learning programs.

Senator Ralph Yarborough's untiring and persistent leadership in the field of education has brought spectacular advances during the 12 years he has served in the Senate. The legacy of his labors will benefit Americans of all ages for many years to come.

Hearings of Senate's Special Committee on Aging, Senator Yarborough and former Senator Maurine Neuberger of Oregon question witness of Food and Drug Administration on fraudulent health practices that endanger health and cost the American consumers a billion dollars annually.

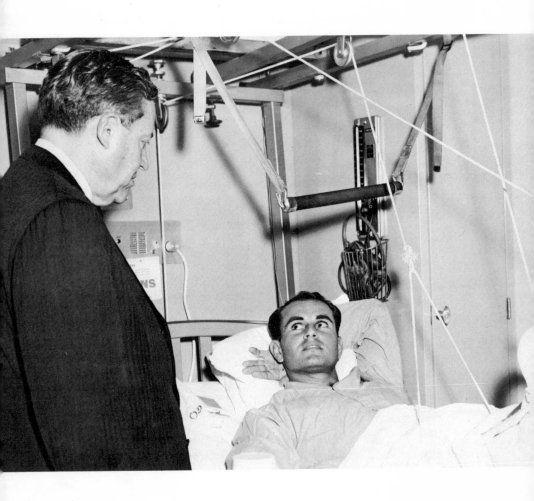

Health Care for Americans

8

YARBOROUGH OF TEXAS became Chairman of the Senate Labor and Public Welfare Committee upon the convening of the 91st Congress in January, 1969. When the Committee itself organized shortly thereafter, he chose to chair the Health Subcommittee, much to the surprise of many sage Capitol Hill observers. Some Senate-watchers had been certain he would assume the chairmanship of the Education Subcommittee, which was also vacant. Others had thought he would hold onto the Labor Subcommittee, which he had chaired so effectively since 1966.

When he opted for the Health Subcommittee, his colleagues, reporters and sages all sought an explanation from Yarborough himself. His candid reply foreshadowed the major emphasis that the Labor and Public Welfare Committee will take into the 1970's under Chairman Yarborough's leadership:

"Many people have asked me why, with my lifelong interest in education, I chose the Chairmanship of the Health Subcommittee in the present Congress when the Education Subcommittee was open to me. My answer is that over the past decade the Congress has done a remarkable job of helping to improve the educational system of our country. Not everything has been solved, but I do believe that we lead the world in providing educational opportunities for our children.

"We do not lead the world in providing health care. For the past eleven years I served on the Health Subcommittee under Lister Hill, most of the time as ranking

109

majority member. That daily contact was bound to rub off. So I took the Chairmanship of the Health Subcommittee to try to help make good health care for every citizen a national goal—then to reach that goal. I want to tackle what I believe to be the biggest domestic problem in this country today."

Chairman Yarborough brought impressive credentials in the health field to back up his announced health priority objectives for the Committee to pursue. Much of his behind-the-scenes work in the Health Subcommittee, following his first assignment to it in 1958, was overshadowed by his notable accomplishments in the educational area. Moreover, the widely-publicized accomplishments of the wise and skillful former Chairman of the Committee—Lister Hill of Alabama—had made Congressional history in the health field over the span of a generation. The sponsor and legislative helmsman of every single health bill to be enacted by Congress since World War II, the kindly Alabaman was nationally known as "Mr. Health." Characteristically, Yarborough sought no personal glory or publicity for his quietly effective work with Hill on the Health Subcommittee. In a decade he observed, learned and ultimately acquired a rare layman's knowledge of such highly technical areas as health research, epidemiology, hospital construction, heart disease, public health disciplines and other complex medical subjects. Yarborough was also one of the earliest Senate backers of Federal family planning legislation. His committee's hearings in the fall of 1969 concentrate on related population control measures. When the Texan was named to the Appropriations Committee in 1965, he bolstered the good medical causes of Senator Hill, who also served as Chairman of the Labor, Health, Education and Welfare Appropriations Subcommittee.

This potent "one-two" punch in the Senate on health legislation was reinforced by aggressive leadership in the House. The late Representative John E. Fogarty of Rhode Island, who was Chairman of the counterpart House Appropriations Subcommittee, was a persuasive House advocate of constructive health proposals. Ralph Yarborough now mans the helm of health leadership in the Congress. Senator Hill retired in 1968 and Congressman Fogarty died on the opening day of the 1967 session—both to the Nation's loss.

A summary of the health legislation passed during the past decade of enlightened Congressional action is awesome—especially in view of Congress' long neglect of health matters—even if we only consider the titles of the major programs enacted. The mere names of these laws tell the story of a Congressional awakening:

85th Congress

1957-58

Hill-Burton Hospital Construction Amendments (P.L. 85-589, 664)

Health Research Facilities Act (P.L. 85-777)

Mentally Retarded Children's Education Act (P.L. 85-926)

Indian Health Construction Act (P.L. 85-151)

Public Health Schools Comprehensive Education Act (P.L. 85-544)

Food Additives Amendments (P.L. 85-929)

86th Congress

1959-60

Public Health Service Training Act and Amendments (P.L. 86-105 and 720)

Pesticide Control Act (P.L. 86-537)

International Health Research Act (P.L. 86-610)

Food Additives Regulation Act (P.L. 86-618)

Air Pollution Control Act Amendments (P.L. 86-365)

Public Health Service Commissioned Corps Personnel Act (P.L. 86-415)

Motor Vehicle Exhaust Study Act (P.L. 86-493)

Public Health Service General Research Grant Act (P.L. 86-798)

87th Congress

1961-62

Community Health Services and Facilities Act (P.L. 87-692, 395)

Food Additives Amendments (P.L. 87-19)

Metal and Nonmetallic Mine Health Study Act (P.L. 87-300)

Vaccination Assistance Act (P.L. 87-868)

Institute of Child Health and Human Development—Institute of General Medical Sciences Act (P.L. 87-838)

88th Congress

1963-64

Health Professions Educational Assistance Act (P.L. 88-129)

Maternal and Child Health Services Amendments (P.L. 88-156)

Air Pollution Control Amendments (P.L. 88-206)

Mental Retardation Facilities and Community Health Centers Construction Act (P.L. 88-164)

Hospital and Medical Facilities Amendments (P.L. 88-443)

Nurse Training Act (P.L. 88-581)

Public Health Schools Comprehensive Education Amendments (P.L. 88-497)

Food Additives Amendments (P.L. 88-625)

Optometry Students Loan Act (P.L. 88-654)

89th Congress

1965-66

Community Health Services Amendments (P.L. 89-109)

Health Research Facilities Amendments (P.L. 89-115)

Medical Library Assistance Act (P.L. 89-232)

Pesticide Research Act (P.L. 89-232)

Older Americans Act (P.L. 89-73)

Drug Abuse Control Amendments (P.L. 89-74)

Health Professions Educational Assistance Amendments (P.L. 89-290)

Heart Disease, Cancer, and Stroke—Regional Medical Programs Act (P.L. 89-239)

112

Senator Yarborough chats with AFL-CIO President George Meany before his testimony in the 90th Congress in support of migrant legislation.

National Technical Institute for the Deaf Act (P.L. 89-36)

Medicare, Social Security Amendments (P.L. 89-97)

Community Mental Health Centers Act (P.L. 89-105)

Comprehensive Health Planning and Public Health Services Act (P.L. 89-749)

Allied Health Professions Personnel Training Act (P.L. 89-751)

Narcotic Addict Rehabilitation Act (P.L. 89-793)

Solid Waste Disposal Act (P.L. 89-272)

Child Nutrition Act (P.L. 89-642)

Neighborhood Health Centers Program—Economic Opportunity Act Amendments (P.L. 89-794)

Food and Drug Consumer Education Act (P.L. 89-756)

Food and Drug Officials Training Act (P.L. 89-755)

Veterinary Medical Education Act (P.L. 89-709)

Vocational Rehabilitation Amendments (P.L. 89-333)

90th Congress

1967-68

Partnership for Health Act (P.L. 90-174)

Mental Retardation Amendments (P.L. 90-170)

Community Health Centers Amendments (P.L. 90-13)

Air Quality Act (P.L. 90-148)

Family Planning Services Act (P.L. 90-248)

Health Manpower Act (P.L. 90-490)

Alcoholic and Narcotic Addict Rehabilitation Amendments; Migrant Agricultural Workers Health Amendments; Regional Medical Amendments; and Solid Waste Disposal Amendments (P.L. 90-574)

National Eye Institute Act (P.L. 90-489)

Vocational Rehabilitation Amendments (P.L. 90-99)

Health Needs

Yet despite these far-reaching health achievements during the past six Congresses, Senator Yarborough is concerned because America shamefully trails most of the advanced nations of the world in a number of the key health indices. The U.S. ranks a lowly 14th among the countries of the world in infant mortality rates. Twenty countries have

Chairman Yarborough meets with distinguished group of Texas medical and dental leaders in 1969 in Houston. At the left are Sumter S. Arnim, D.D.S., Ph.-D., Dean, Graduate School of Biomedical Sciences, Division of Graduate Studies, University of Texas Dental Branch and Dr. Michael E. DeBakey, Baylor College of Medicine. To the right are Dr. R. Lee Clark, President, M. D. Anderson Hospital and Tumor Institute, Joseph L. Melnick, Ph.D., and Carlton F. Hazlewood, Ph.D., both of the Baylor College of Medicine.

Below, Tigua Indians of El Paso serenaded Yarborough on a recent visit to his Washington office. Left to right, they are Jose Granillo, Trinidad Granillo, and Miguel Pedraza. Yarborough has been a Senate leader in the fight for better health programs for both Indians and migrants.

higher life expectancy rates for males; eleven countries have longer-lived females than we do. The U.S. has the highest incidence of death from heart disease among males between 40 and 50 years of age of any advanced country reporting its health statistics to the United Nations. We walked on the moon before the Russians, but the average Russian walks longer on earth than the average American.

Senator Yarborough recently pointed out that "the American people, during the year 1968, spent some $53 billion through public taxation and private payments on medical care and treatment." This sum is about six percent of our entire gross national product. The Public Health Service estimates that within the next few years, our multitude of health services will be America's largest employer of manpower. Already, the so-called "health service industry" employs more than 3½ million persons. This does not include some 1 million others currently engaged in the manufacture and distribution of drugs. Employment in the health industry, as a category of livelihood today, is exceeded by only two other industries—agriculture and construction.

"In America," Yarborough says, "we have a concept of a health industry, not health care. The Nation has not yet accepted a concept of health care for our people; the question of illness is treated as a business for profit."

The blunt Texan's damning indictment of the level of our present health standards is a shockingly accurate appraisal of our current situation. During his 1958 campaign for the Senate, Yarborough used a slogan: "Let's put the jam on the lower shelf so the little people can reach it." Now, as Chairman of the Labor and Public Welfare Committee, he is saying, in effect: "Let's put health services on the lower shelf so that all Americans may have their fair share of modern, enlightened medical care."

Many alarms ringing over the past decade have helped arouse the concern of the average citizen to critical matters of health. He is bombarded daily by warnings of cancer caused by smoking or breathing polluted air, of the danger to him from chemical pesticides contained in the food he eats, of suffering a heart attack because of his fatty diet, his lack of exercise or the stress of his job.

Yet the average American today can expect to live longer than his father or his grandfather. During the past three generations, life expectancy has increased by about 20 years. This remarkable longevity increase, as Yarborough has pointed out, is due primarily to advances in medical research. By mass vaccination, we have been able virtually to eliminate the incidence of premature death from smallpox, typhoid, diphtheria, measles and other infectious diseases that only yesterday took such a heavy toll. Effective vaccines and drugs against polio, tuberculosis, pneumonia and many respiratory infections have added to the average U.S. life span.

Americans are learning, however, that deaths are rising sharply from other such dread diseases as cancer, multiple sclerosis, muscular dystrophy, leukemia, heart disease, emphysema and cystic fibrosis. The crash medical research program spearheaded by the National Institutes of Health has dedicatedly tackled these and other serious diseases. Much progress has been made through the investment of public funds in NIH—some $1.4 billion in fiscal year 1969. This is 40 percent of all funds spent in the U.S. on medical research.

"We must develop the same sense of urgency with regard to chronic long-term killers and cripplers as we have in conquering infectious diseases," Chairman Yarborough asserts. When the Nixon Administration's health budget was sent to Congress in April 1969, instead of the badly-needed increase in funds, it swung a meat-ax cut of $50 million at the National Institutes of Health budget for carrying on research programs to find the cause and cure for the major killer diseases. Overall, the Nixon budget recommended a slash of almost $750 million in health and related programs for Fiscal Year 1970.

Yarborough leveled a broadside at the proposed cuts:

"Do we have the answer to heart disease, which kills one million Americans every year? Do we have the answer to cancer, which kills one American every two minutes? The Administration must think we do, because it has cut the budget for the National Heart Institute $6 million under last year's inadequate figure and the National Cancer Institute by $5 million less than was appropriated last year."

But finding money for research—important as it is—is only a part of the health care problem in the United States. Yarborough is convinced that the entire health profession is growingly aware of the fact that adequate health care has moved in the public mind from "a privilege to a right." He believes that such care should be available on the basis of need, not income. He feels that this requires an entire new concept of health care on the part of professionals as well as a restructuring of Federal programs in order to maximize the *delivery* of essential health services to all citizens.

Yarborough has pinpointed the major problem areas with which his Committee must deal if national health goals are to be achieved:

On the doctor shortage—

"The shortage of doctors in this country is a national scandal. Each year, this great and affluent nation *imports* 2,000 doctors from foreign countries to make up for the demanding deficiencies in our health education system."

"By way of contrast, the Soviet Union has 600,000 doctors—twice the number we have—and it *exports* 2,000 doctors to the under-developed countries of the world each year."

"We cannot staff our 7,000 hospitals with American-trained doctors. It may seem incredible, but we have never stated how many doctors we really need!"

Yarborough and other pleased members of the Senate and House Committees joined in the bill signing ceremony with President Kennedy marking the enactment of the Mental Retardation Facilities and Community Health Centers Construction Act of 1963.

"We need at least 200 medical schools in this country, but are now staggering slowly toward a limited goal of 100 medical schools . . . 900 of 1,300 qualified medical school applicants in Texas alone were turned away last year because of the limited capacity of Texas' four medical schools."

On the lack of adequate health insurance protection—

"Despite three decades of effort by our commercial insurance companies and Blue Cross-Blue Shield, 30 million Americans still have *no* health insurance at all . . . *two-thirds of the costs* of personal health care in America are still uninsured . . . even Medicare pays only 40 percent of the total medical bills of the average elderly person."

On health manpower requirements—

"We need 50,000 more physicians than we now have. We need 80,000 more registered nurses and 42,000 more practical nurses. In 1966, hospitals employed 360,000 registered nurses and needed 22 percent more. They employed 150,000 practical nurses and needed 27 percent more to provide optimum care."

"In 1950, 2.3 percent of the whole national labor force was engaged in medical employment. By 1960, it was 3.7 percent of the labor force, accounting for 3 million persons. By 1975, it is estimated that more than 4 percent of persons gainfully employed will be working to provide for the health needs of the American people."

On hunger and malnutrition—

"It is within our power to banish hunger and malnutrition from our land; we have a responsibility to exercise that power. Our unparalleled agricultural abundance must be shared with all our people here at home—no American should be malnourished."

"The problem of malnutrition is most tragic in the young. Experts say that by age 4, about 90 percent of a child's brain growth has occurred. It is during these tender years that a lack of proper nutrition is most dangerous. Malnutrition at this age easily can cause mental retardation, irreversible in later years."

On construction and renovation of hospital facilities—

"Our hospitals are badly in need of substantial financial assistance for construction and modernization. Figures show that the 50 States report urgent needs for construction of new health facilities costing $5 billion and urgent needs for modernization or replacement of obsolete health care facilities costing an additional $11 billion now. These needs cannot be met without additional Federal help."

"Congress authorized $195 million for hospital construction and modernization for Fiscal Year 1970, but the Nixon Administration is asking only $50 million, or one dollar out of four. . . . . In Texas, the need for Federal assistance in this field has been 4 or 5 times greater than the amount the State has been allocated in grants."

Many have asked the logical, multi-billion dollar question: What are the chances for successful achievement of these dramatic increases in funds and medical manpower that are required if our national health objectives are to be fulfilled? In essence, the question usually is asked like this:

Granting the political facts of life in Washington and the way things are accomplished in this high-powered, public relations-oriented field—Why hasn't the need for health care by the American people been "glamorized" like some of our missile systems or "dramatized" like the space program in order to "sell" the health program to the public and thereby to the politically-sensitive Congress and the Administration?

Perhaps the best answer to this classic political-public relations question was given by Senator Yarborough in May 1969 in remarks to the 20th Anniversary Albert Lasker Medical Journal Awards Luncheon in New York. He said:

> "There are no big, fat hundred million dollars involved in contract after contract for health programs—like the Defense Department hands out; nothing like the contracts in the hundreds of millions for space launchers or missiles. The needed health care program is only about people; we have got to stir people up to demand it."

Mobilizing for Action

Chairman Ralph Yarborough is himself taking the lead in "stirring people up." Just as he did in his first hectic campaigns in Texas in the 1950's, he has taken to the platforms throughout the country to deliver major speeches on our health crisis—teaching, preaching, pleading, cajoling his audiences to get behind the drive for decent health care for our citizens. As part of his evangelic effort to focus public attention on the Nation's medical and health needs, Yarborough has resorted to two approaches—(1) he introduced a

President Johnson presents ceremonial pen to his fellow Texan after signing into law the Community Mental Health Centers Act of 1965, one of almost two dozen major health measures enacted during the 89th Congress. Yarborough played a leading role in these health achievements.

whole series of health bills to pinpoint specific areas that demand legislative action and (2) he initiated extensive hearings by his Health Subcommittee on the quality and quantity of health care now available or which should be available in our country.

Another significant health-related contribution by Yarborough was his prompt establishment of the special Subcommittee on Alcoholism and Narcotics to aid in the fight against the root-causes of crime in the U.S. The Subcommittee is chaired by Iowa Senator Harold E. Hughes.

Bills sponsored or co-sponsored by Chairman Yarborough in the 91st Congress cover virtually every dimension of the health field:

—Community Mental Health Centers Amendments
—Occupational Health and Safety Act
—Communicable Disease Control Amendments
—Migrant Health Act Amendments
—Medical Library and Health Communications Assistance Amendments
—International Health, Education and Labor Act
—Hospital and Medical Facilities Construction and Modernization Amendments
—Environmental Quality Improvement Act
—National Lung Institute Act
—Medicare Drug Provision and $50 Deductible Repeal Amendments
—Public Health School Assistance Amendments
—Medical School Construction Assistance Amendments
—Drug Abuse Control Amendments
—Coal Mine Health Act
—Developmental Disabilities Services Act

Many of Yarborough's Senate colleagues who share his concern for our health needs have joined in backing most of these measures.

Laws authorizing more than a dozen existing health programs are due to expire during the 1969-70 session of the

123

91st Congress. This fact provides an excellent opportunity for Yarborough's Committee to reexamine the scope and effectiveness of the health measures presently in force. It also gives the Committee a golden opportunity to develop a broadly coordinated approach to the entire roster of health programs in which the Federal government is now involved.

Health Care for All

Senator Ralph Yarborough has already fired the opening salvos in the battle to make the national goal of good health care a reality for every American. In his usual straightforward fashion, he says:

"If we can afford a war in Vietnam that is costing us $36 billion a year, then we can surely afford some sort of national health insurance for all our people. Good health is not a luxury—it is as basic as food, clothing and shelter, and it should be guaranteed to every American through a national program of health insurance."

Yarborough has pointed out that the idea of national health insurance is not exactly new. It was recommended to Congress by former President Truman 20 years ago. After that, it took 17 more years even to enact the Medicare program, which Yarborough believes to be only a bare minimum of what the American people need in health care insurance protection.

The Senator has summed up the dimensions of America's health problem by pointing out that "it is not a lack of knowledge that is responsible for America's lagging behind other nations of the world in health care. It is not our medical science, but our *system* that is sorely deficient." Yarborough goes on to assert that "we must bring the *delivery* of health care up to the standard of our knowledge in health sciences; otherwise the money spent on health research by the taxpayers will not benefit the average citizen." He concludes:

"We need medicine that is a service for people, as distinguished from medicine for money. We need to restudy the structure of the medical care industry with this objective in mind."

Senator Ralph Yarborough has precisely defined his health legislation goal and proclaimed his determination to attain it:

"I intend, as long as I am a member of the Senate and as long as I remain on this good earth, to fight for the day when good health care for all Americans will be a reality. I cannot do it alone, nor can the Congress do it alone. We will not succeed until the American people support us, and demand that we allocate money to health as we are now allocating it to space and to the arms race."

Few who know Ralph Yarborough and his "bull dog" reputation in the Senate for legislative perseverance doubt that this national goal of good health that he seeks for all citizens will one day be achieved. Nor that the Senator, as long as he is "on this good earth," will continue to fight for it.

9

A Gallery of Legislative Achievement

DURING HIS 12 YEARS OF SERVICE in the United States Senate, Senator Ralph W. Yarborough has himself sponsored scores of legislative proposals, a large number of which have been enacted. He has co-sponsored practically all of the domestic programs that flowed from the activism of the Kennedy-Johnson years.

Each bill that is introduced has a worthy objective in the mind of its sponsor. The push and pull of the legislative process, as it comes to bear on the bill, acts to measure a bill's worthiness in terms of broad national interest or as local or State needs may dictate. The Congressional committee system provides the machinery for measuring a given legislative need against other competing needs. These legislative needs are parceled out, of course, under the jurisdictional responsibilities established under Senate and House rules that govern committee arrangements.

Legislative Mill

Few of the legislative proposals introduced in Congress survive the rigors of the complex system. An astonishing total of some 25,000 bills were offered in the Senate and House of Representatives during the 90th Congress. Less than 700 of these bills—roughly three per cent of all introduced—were finally enacted into law before adjournment. Much creative, progressive legislation fell by the wayside, along with many ill-conceived measures. It is to the credit of the committee system that most of the "bad" bills die young, although the definition of "bad" is likely to vary considerably with one's political or economic persuasion.

Members of Congress generally have primary legislative interests—stemming from their personal bent as well as the nature of their constituencies—that closely parallel their Committee assignments. In a sense, the Committee system evolves a body of legislative specialists in each of the many complicated fields in which Congress passes laws. Thus we find in Congress housing authorities, immigration experts, missile authorities, education specialists, health authorities, atomic energy specialists, banking experts and dozens of other specialized legislators.

Yarborough's Versatility

Ralph Yarborough's legislative career is rare in Congressional annals because his range of active legislative participation has reached far beyond the confined jurisdictions of the various committees on which he has served. This may be attributed, in part, to the broad reach of his knowledge and the great diversity of his lifetime experiences. His versatility also reflects to some extent the many areas of activity of the 11 million people of Texas. The fields of their endeavor encompass farming and ranching, international trade, electronics and aerospace industries, oil and chemical production and hundreds of other commercial and industrial fields. In particular, service on the Appropriations Committee invariably tends to broaden a Senator's interests because of his responsibility in weighing national priorities against State or regional needs in the annual allocation of Federal funds to implement ongoing programs. Even many billions of dollars can be parceled out in only so many ways.

Former Committee Chairman Hill characterized Yarborough's wide field of legislative endeavor when he said:

"Champion of America's veterans, defender of the working man, the farmer, the young and the old, leader in the struggle for Federal aid to education, and ardent supporter of every effort to improve the Nation's health, Senator Ralph Yarborough in his service on the Senate Committee on Labor and Public Welfare has proved himself one of our most diligent energetic, determined, and effective Members."

To illustrate the wide range of the Texas Senator's legislative activity, a series of thumb-nail portraits of his achievement is apt at this point. These merely touch upon some of the major fields in which Yarborough has made lasting and significant contributions to Texas and the Nation as a whole.

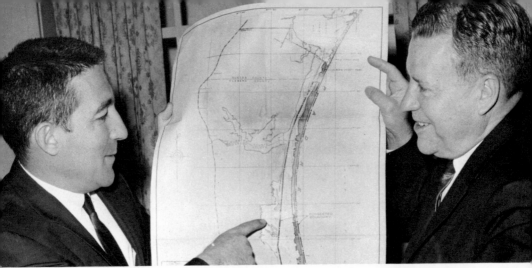

Former Interior Secretary Stewart Udall and Senator Yarborough discuss Padre Island National Seashore boundary plans. Yarborough's long, four-year fight for enactment of the Padre Island bill was finally won in 1962.

CONSERVATION

Ralph Yarborough is an ardent conservationist. An all-round outdoorsman, he has been one of the Senate's most vigorous advocates of the wise preservation and public enjoyment of our natural wonders and resources. His four-year legislative fight made the Padre Island National Seashore Recreation Area—a 74 mile-long strand off Texas' Gulf Coast—a reality in 1962. With the Padre Island bill enacted, Yarborough turned to creating the Guadalupe Mountains National Park, enacted in 1966. Yarborough has co-sponsored stringent water and air pollution control laws. He has supported Job Corps Conservation Centers as well as being a tireless advocate of multi-purpose dams and water conservation programs.

Bills to establish the Big Thicket National Park, Dinosaur Trail National Monument and the Amistad National Recreation Area have been introduced by Yarborough during the past several Congresses and are moving closer to passage. His successful conservation proposals include the Golden Eagle protection law, the Fort Davis National Monument and the Alibates Flint Quarries National Monument. He is the Senate leader for legislation to prevent the commercial importation of endangered species of wildlife from foreign countries.

Yarborough discusses soil conservation program with young Texas farmer.

AGRICULTURE

Almost three-quarters of a million Texans live on farms and ranches, while another two million reside in small towns and rural areas of the State. Yarborough's own rural upbringing in East Texas makes him instinctively attuned to the needs and problems of farm families in Texas and throughout the country. The growth of giant "agribusiness" has caused serious economic dislocations, affecting family farms and rural communities. The Senator has worked to help offset the effects of this agricultural upheaval through the enactment of rural housing programs, commodity price supports, soil conservation programs and agricultural research. He has also supported low-interest loans through the Farmers' Home Administration and the Great Plains Conservation Program. He has backed many water-system and small watershed projects as well as on-the-farm training programs under the Cold War GI Bill and rural development programs through the Economic Development Act and the Economic Opportunity Act.

A long-time supporter of the Rural Electrification Act, the Senator has worked to help meet the ever-expanding power demands of rural areas. In particular, his efforts on the Agriculture Appropriations Subcommittee have helped to obtain needed R.E.A. funds to implement this and other important farm programs.

CITIES

Three of every four Texans live with the problems of an urban environment. The cancer-like overgrowth of our Nation's cities has therefore drawn a major part of Senator Yarborough's boundless legislative energies. During his years in the Senate, Yarborough backed a host of new laws that have launched the most comprehensive attack on urban blight in the history of any country. These measures include air and water pollution abatement laws, public and elderly housing programs, the Rent Supplement and Model Cities programs and crime control measures. The Senator has been a mainstay of Congressional action for public facility construction grants and loans to municipalities. Yarborough has been a persistent advocate of local public works programs to improve our urban highways and mass transportation systems, environmental health measures, programs to train the unemployed and to provide for acquisition of "open-space" land.

Yarborough has long backed and seen to reality the establishment of neighborhood health services in poverty areas, the modernization of our airports, expanded hospital construction and the juvenile delinquency control program. He has co-sponsored virtually every such urban assistance measure acted upon by Congress since his election to the Senate in 1957.

Yarborough has also pioneered in sponsoring legislation that would financially compensate the victims of crime. He was also a strong supporter of the Law Enforcement Assistance Act of 1965 and the Omnibus Crime Control and Safe Streets Act of 1968.

State Representative Lauro Cruz of Houston (left) and U.S. Congressman Bob Eckhardt (right) join Senator Yarborough on a walking tour of Houston neighborhoods to observe health needs.

POVERTY

Texas has the dubious distinction of having more citizens existing below the poverty level than are found in any other State in the Nation. The vicious cycle of generation-to-generation poverty still stalks the *barrios* of Mexican border cities and the rural areas of East Texas and the Plains.

As a member of the Poverty Subcommittee Senator Yarborough co-sponsored the original Economic Opportunity Act of 1964 and remains a staunch advocate of former President Johnson's "war on poverty." Job training programs for young people from all across the country have been carried out by the highly successful Job Corps facilities at Camp Gary. The McKinney Women's Job Corps Center and the New Waverly Conservation Center have also given thousands of underprivileged a chance to make better, more productive lives for themselves.

Texas' senior Senator has supported Headstart programs for preschool children, a variety of local community action projects and migrant labor programs. He initiated the Bilingual Education program to help crack the language barrier that perpetuates the poverty cycle. But the "war on poverty" is far from won. Defense priorities have sadly restricted the amount of public funds available to make a more sizable impact on the grimly ironic problem of poverty amidst plenty in America.

Army Reserve Colonel Yarborough during an inspection of military installation in Vietnam during Southeast Asian trip in November, 1968, found a touch of home in the Mekong Delta.

DEFENSE

Ralph Yarborough has consistently sought to match our national defense effort to the dimensions of the threat of attack and, accordingly, to maintain our military strength and our system of defense pacts with the Western-aligned nations of Europe and Asia. Not inconsistently, he has often stated that "world problems cannot be resolved by relying on military solutions alone."

A full-time Senatorial civilian, but a part-time Army reserve officer, Colonel Yarborough has toured the battlefronts of Vietnam and our defense installations in Europe and Korea. His concern for the well-being of American servicemen sparked his long and successful fight to enact the Cold War GI Bill. He also co-sponsored and helped push through the Career Military Pay Raise Acts of 1958 and 1963.

Yarborough's earlier leadership as Chairman of the Veterans' Affairs Subcommittee resulted in more than a dozen laws bearing his name. These bills improved veterans' pensions and disability compensation, their hospital care and benefits for their widows and orphans. The War Orphans' Educational Act is just one example of Yarborough's deep concern for the tragic aftermath of war.

Senator Ralph Yarborough discusses 88th Congress tax reform bill with Senate Majority Whip Humphrey. Yarborough was active supporter of tax cut measure and has worked for further reforms in the 91st Congress.

TAX REFORM

Yarborough has advocated sorely needed income tax reform ever since his 1957 election to the Senate. In his first year in Washington he fought unsuccessfully to raise personal income tax exemptions from $600 to $800 in order to benefit low and middle-income taxpayers. He supported income and excise tax reductions during the Johnson Administration.

In the 91st Congress Yarborough has favored broad tax reforms, including a drastic increase in personal exemptions from $600 to $1,200, plus the closing of glaring tax loopholes that benefit high-income groups who pay no taxes and other special interests. He has also co-sponsored legislation to levy an Excess War Profits Tax. In 1969 Yarborough opposed extension of the 10 percent tax surcharge on the income of all citizens, and he has advocated repeal of the inflation-feeding 7 percent investment tax credit.

President Nixon presents to Senator Yarborough the ceremonial pen used to sign into law the Construction Safety Act of 1969, one of the first bills to be steered through Yarborough's Senate Labor and Public Welfare Committee in the 91st Congress.

LABOR

When Ralph Yarborough became Chairman of the Senate Labor Subcommittee in the spring of 1966, his first duty was to steer through the very intricate and controversial minimum wage bill. He was the floor manager of the measure that was passed by the Senate in August of that year and then signed into law by President Johnson. The Fair Labor Standards Act Amendments of 1966 was the most significant improvement in the law since its New Deal passage in 1938. It raised the minimum wage from $1.25 an hour to the present $1.60, expanded the types of industries covered under the Act and dramatically brought some 400,000 agricultural workers under minimum wage protection for the first time. The new law also hiked minimum pay for some 9 million persons in retail trades, laundries, restaurants, hospitals, hotels, construction jobs and educational institutions. Such workers, like their agricultural counterparts, had never been legally accorded coverage under the minimum wage umbrella.

Ever in the forefront of constructive labor legislation, Yarborough has also been a co-sponsor of laws covering manpower training programs, vocational training, occupational safety and other measures improving the economic status of American wage earners.

U.S. Delegates to Interparliamentary Union Conference in Tehran, Iran in 1966 included three Texans—Senator Ralph Yarborough, Congressman Jim Wright of Fort Worth (far left), and Congressman Bob Poage of Waco (right).

FOREIGN POLICY

Although not a member of the Senate Foreign Relations Committee, Senator Ralph Yarborough has taken a keen interest in international affairs. His work in Europe with the American Chamber of Commerce in Berlin made him aware of the importance of a thriving international trade to our domestic economy. He has served on the Commerce subcommittees on trade with Latin America and Africa and has consistently supported U.S. trade fairs and tourist bureaus abroad.

In keeping with his international outlook, Yarborough was a co-sponsor of the precedent-making Peace Corps Act and supported the Food for Peace Program, the Alliance for Progress in Latin America, and the Trade Expansion Act of 1962. He also backed the many Foreign Aid programs, the ratification of the Nuclear Test Ban Treaty and the Nuclear Nonproliferation Treaty. The Senator endorsed the El Chamizal Treaty that settled a minor but century-long border dispute with Mexico.

Senator Yarborough has been appointed on six occasions as a U.S. delegate to international meetings of the Interparliamentary Union, the oldest intergovernmental organization in the world, predating by many years the bygone League of Nations.

AMISTAD DAM

Senator Yarborough addresses crowd gathered for the ceremonial pouring of the first bucket of concrete for construction of the Amistad Dam on the Rio Grande, July 31, 1965. The joint Mexican-United States project has now been completed and was officially opened in 1969.

NATURAL RESOURCES

Yarborough has helped to enact many laws strengthening the fishing and maritime commerce industries of Texas. He authored new bills to free Texas shrimpers from unreasonable restrictions, and he once traveled to Mexico City to help secure more equitable treatment for the Gulf Coast shrimp fleet in what the U.S. regarded as free-fishing international waters.

One-time seaman-student Yarborough has long advocated expansion of the American merchant fleet as well as sponsoring improvements of the Gulf Intra-Coastal Waterway and the improvement of Texas' Gulf Coast port facilities. A yearly concern is working to improve hurricane and flood protection on the Gulf and for flood control dams in Texas' river basins.

When disasters such as floods or hurricane winds and tides brought wholesale human loss and property destruction, Yarborough acted promptly to request all Federal relief assistance available under the law. He is still pressing some of the claims that the Federal government has not yet reimbursed.

Federal Communications Commissioner T. A. M. Craven and Senator Yarborough examine model of communications satellite.

COMMUNICATIONS

Throughout his career in the Capital, Senator Yarborough has been one of the Senate's most articulate defenders of the public interest against monopolistic influence. In Congress it is an old truism that men can be judged partly on the basis of the enemies they make. Texas' Yarborough has found some powerful adversaries. His service on the Senate Commerce Committee and its Freedom of Communications Subcommittee has brought him into conflict with several corporate communications giants on occasion. In 1962 he helped lead an eight-week filibuster to block American Telephone & Telegraph's domination of a public communications satellite corporation, now known as Comsat. The Senate finally voted "cloture" to cut off debate on the bill and it eventually passed. This was the first time since 1927 that the Senate had knocked down its own zealously-guarded prerogative of unlimited debate. As finally enacted, however, the measure sharply limited communication company control of Comsat.

Yarborough also opposed AT&T plans to raise telephone rates in 1963 by some 82 percent on person-to-person long-distance calls. Since Texas is the only State without a State regulatory body for phone rates, Yarborough protested the plan to the Federal Communications Commission, which held hearings on the AT&T proposal. The AT&T application for a rate increase was subsequently withdrawn.

Yarborough's Commerce Committee held hearings in 1960 on legislation instigated by TV networks to repeal the "equal time" provisions of the law. Such a repeal would, for example, permit televised debates of major party Presidential candidates without offering time to other candidates. Senator Yarborough questioned TV network executives about discriminatory practices and the selection policies used in scheduling various public officials' appearances on nationwide panel programs. The anti-equal-time bill was subsequently set aside.

Yarborough discusses ways to improve Federal-State relations with State Representatives Lauro Cruz and Curtis Graves during a visit to Washington.

AGED

Senator Yarborough's work on the Labor Subcommittee during the 90th Congress was instrumental in the enactment of the Age Discrimination in Employment Act of 1967. This law prohibits job discrimination against workers in the 40 to 65 year age bracket. The Texan also serves on the Special Committee on Aging, which conducted extensive hearings into the problem of age barriers in employment. These committee studies inspired Yarborough's sponsorship of the Middle-Aged and Older Workers Full Employment bill. This new measure invokes creative solutions to the problems of age through retraining and education, research and demonstration projects, and community senior service programs.

Yarborough's effective action for America's senior citizens was highlighted by his work to help enact the Medicare program. He has recently pushed to improve the program by extending its benefits to cover the cost of drugs and by eliminating its present $50 deductible provision covering medical bills.

Saturn V space vehicle carrying Apollo 8 Astronauts Borman, Lovell and Anders lifts off the launching pad at Cape Kennedy on its historic moon orbital mission, December 21, 1968.

SPACE

Ralph Yarborough is proud of the spectacular accomplishments that have enabled America to surpass the Soviet space efforts. Like many people all over the world, he watched and was awed by the historic landing of our astronauts on the moon's surface.

He is especially proud of the role that Texas and Texans have played in our space exploration program, in which the Manned Space Center in Houston is such a vital link. Ever since his early support of the National Aeronautics and Space Act and the National Defense Education Act in 1958, he has worked diligently in helping to move our scientific space effort onward and upward toward the mysteries of the universe. As Yarborough said in praise of our astronauts:

"We honor them in all the ways that men honor great and brave and noble achievements. They have opened a highway to the stars."

Mrs. S. E. Bartley, sister of the late Speaker Sam Rayburn, joins Senator Yarborough and Congressman Jack Brooks of Beaumont at the dedication of the Sam Rayburn Dam and Reservoir on the Lower Neches River, in East Texas on May 8, 1965.

PUBLIC WORKS

Public works projects to stimulate the economic as well as human development of Texas and the Nation have been another major area of Senator Yarborough's legislative concern. He supported the Public Works and Economic Development Act of 1965 and its forerunner, the Area Redevelopment Act of 1961. Both of these programs have pumped Federal funds into essential projects in dozens of economically distressed Texas communities and rural areas. In the 91st Congress he has advocated enactment of the Southwestern Human Development Act. Appropriately named, this measure would provide special education, job training, health and leadership programs to raise the living standards and aspirations of all Mexican-Americans in the Southwest.

Yarborough backs Texas' Trinity River project, the State's small watershed development and various other water projects such as the Sam Rayburn Dam, the Sanford Dam on the Canadian River and the Amistad Dam on the Rio Grande. Today these projects provide irrigation, navigation, flood control and recreation benefits to millions of people in Texas and the Nation. He has also worked to push through Federal grants for construction of municipal sewage treatment plants and was a co-sponsor of the Saline Water Conservation Act.

Former Postmaster General John A. Gronouski presents to Senator Yarborough the artist's design of the Sam Houston commemorative stamp.

POST OFFICE

During his 12 years of service on the Senate Post Office and Civil Service Committee, Ralph Yarborough has worked for every law enacted to give comparability to the wage and salary levels of America's postal and classified civil service employees. He has fought to improve retirement pensions, fringe benefits and working conditions of those presently employed by the Federal government, and he has worked to liberalize the retirement annuities of those already retired.

As the ranking Democrat on this Committee, Yarborough advocates reform of the whole structure of Federal employee-management relations, including more adequate grievance procedures. He has also urged a greater capital investment and increased research and development funds for the postal establishment to meet the fantastic increase in the annual mail load. Yarborough has consistently fought for a more equitable postal rate structure, with costs distributed fairly among the various classes of mail users.

Famous consumer advocate Ralph Nader chats with Senator Yarborough before testifying in support of the Texan's Occupational Health and Safety bill during the 90th Congress.

CONSUMERS

The problems of people—of consumers buying in the marketplace or citizens dealing with their government—occupy a prominent place in each of Senator Ralph Yarborough's long legislative days. The Senator is visited by thousands of his Texas constituents each year. Thousands of letters are handled each month by Senator Yarborough and his competent staff. Many of the inquiries involve murky problems such as pension claims, immigration questions, military hardships, small business assistance, or the many impasses that people may encounter with governmental bureaucracy. Other constituents call or write to express their views on legislation, government policies or programs. Yarborough welcomes and encourages the broad exercise of such Constitutional rights by all citizens.

His other Senate duties affect the general well-being in a number of ways. Yarborough co-sponsored almost all major bills enacted during recent years to protect the American consumer. He has, for example, supported the so-called Truth in Lending Act, Drug Industry Regulation Act and the Highway Safety Act. His mark is on the consumer-guarding Fair Packaging and Labeling Act as well as similar measures such as the Flammable Fabrics Act, the National Commission on Product Safety, the Wholesome Meat Act and the Wholesome Poultry Act.

Ralph Yarborough has often been called the "people's Senator" because of his long demonstrated concern for the people of Texas and the United States as a whole. Nothing pleases him more than to hear a constituent refer to him as "my Senator." He does not regard Texans as blocs of votes or groups having narrow interests, but as individual citizens—each having independent judgment that transcends selfish considerations.

As the late University of Texas Professor J. Frank Dobie once said about Yarborough:

> "The only gain he has ever sought, consistently or inconsistently, has been public gain. He does not try to milk the public for private profit. He seeks the good of people. Nor is his consideration of humanity provincial-minded. . . .
>
> "Every man and every woman is judged by his or her sense of values. Whenever the majority of others in any democracy have a high sense of values, that country will have become a Utopia. When values of life—values beyond money, values that express civilization, enlightenment and justice for the human race come up, we can count on Senator Ralph Yarborough to stand for those values."

In sum, Ralph Yarborough's whole public career reflects an abiding interest in the "common man"—whether as a consumer, a small businessman, a farmer or worker. He believes as did Abraham Lincoln, who first said:

> "God must have loved the common people; He made so many of them!"

Senator and Mrs. Yarborough received enthusiastic welcome on arrival in San Antonio at Ralph W. Yarborough Day at the Hemisphere Exposition, July 31, 1968.

Former Ambassador Edward Clark and Senator Yarborough acknowledge crowd's cheers in a typical Texas parade.

10
The Eyes of
Texas Are Upon Him

IN HIS FIRST TWELVE YEARS in the Senate, Ralph Yarborough has accomplished more than most lawmakers hope to do in a lifetime. But much of the Yarborough story has yet to be written. His influence in the Senate as well as his leadership role in critical American problem areas is likely to be in the ascendant during the 1970's.

The Senator has proved to the people of Texas and the Nation that a courageous and progressive political leader can successfully challenge the most powerful forces of political and economic reaction. He proved that the progressive platform and programs of the national Democratic Party are just as valid and viable in Texas as in the rest of the country. The Texan's election to the Senate in 1957 and his subsequent re-election victories in 1958 and 1964 gave heart to other progressive Democratic candidates in Texas. Yarborough blazed the trail and others will follow him into public office in the years ahead.

Impact on Texas Politics

Yarborough has not only accurately gauged the winds of political change blowing across Texas, he has been a prime mover in instituting those changes. More than anyone else, Yarborough has been able to unify Texas' fiercely independent progressive elements through the force of his personality and vigorous leadership ability. There is no mystery to the "Yarborough coalition." It is made up of the same basic alignment that has given the Democratic Party its strength over the past half-century—small farmers and ranchers, blue collar workers of trade unions, small businessmen, people of minority groups, rural electric cooperative members, the young and the old, teachers, nurses and other professional people, and community leaders from all walks of life. All have the common goal of social and economic progress, a higher standard of living for all Americans and a better life for their families today and for generations to come.

Senator Ralph Yarborough's success at the polls has been a combination of his own dedication and drive and the loyalty and hard work of the Texans who have labored in the political vineyards for Yarborough victories. Their efforts have offset the influence and money that Yarborough's opponents have always brandished and spent in abundance.

Yarborough election victories have come despite formidible obstacles that have loomed on every campaign horizon. There was, of course the familiar lack of campaign funds to wage the same kind of "glamorous" Statewide race that is the trademark of the "millionaire candidate" whom Yarborough usually draws as his primary and general election adversary. But Texas is also famous for its "rough and tumble" political campaigns. Yarborough has been a favorite target of "whisper campaigns" and "smear tactics" that have tried to label him as "a tool of labor," or other epithets. Most Texas voters have not been fooled by such desperate anti-Yarborough smear tactics. They have re-elected him twice by overwhelming margins.

Two totally unrelated incidents—30 years apart—were instrumental in helping to shape Ralph Yarborough's political destiny. The first was back in 1928, when Yarborough was fresh out of the University of Texas Law School. Anxious to get off to a flying start as a lawyer, Ralph had mused aloud to his fiancee, Opal Warren, about running for County Attorney in his native Henderson County. Opal promptly put her foot down on the idea. "If you run," she told Ralph, "the wedding is off. I won't marry a man in politics." Ralph set the idea of politics aside, joined the El Paso law firm and married Opal. Not until 1938, Opal having long since changed her mind, did Yarborough throw his hat into the ring in the race for Texas Attorney General. Today, the Senator counts Opal Warren Yarborough as one of his greatest political assets, and she is indisputably one of the most able campaigners of all senatorial wives.

The second incident that had such an important impact on Yarborough and other Texas progressives occurred during the mud and the fury of the 1958 campaign, after Yarborough's first year in the Senate. His old political enemies, the "Shivercrat" remnants, were determined to blast him out of office before he could have time to solidify his popularity with rank-and-file Texas voters. The self-styled Texas "regulars" ran wealthy Bill Blakley, the former interim Senator, against Yarborough. At the crucial point in the campaign, they played what they believed was their high trump card. The Dallas *Morning News* duly accused Yarborough of receiving some $25,000 in campaign contributions from labor unions. Yarborough's opponents felt confident that this "terrible revelation" would be the "kiss of death," as indeed such disclosures had proved in earlier elections for progressive Democratic candidates in the State. Yarborough smiled and counterpunched. He retorted candidly that the *News* had actually understated the amount of labor's contributions to his campaign. Pointing out that his opponent was a well-known millionaire, he appealed for even more campaign contributions from the "little people" for whom he was fighting! This dramatic political turn-around confounded his opponents and helped produce the smashing victory he scored in the primary over Blakley and led to Yarborough's unprecedented landslide re-election in November, 1958 for a full six-year term in the Senate.

During the next five busy years, Yarborough achieved significant legislative victories in the State as a strong supporter of the progressive Kennedy-Johnson program. In October 1963 his friends and supporters staged a gala "Statewide Texas Salute to Senator Ralph Yarborough," in Austin. In his message to the gathering, the late President John F. Kennedy said:

> "I could talk about some of the things that Ralph Yarborough has done, about his work in education, education for all Americans, for veterans, for hospital care under social security, for an income tax cut to stimulate our economy and provide jobs for our people, for the nuclear test ban treaty—a step towards peace—for human liberties, for the goals that bind Democrats together in this State and all over the Union."

Kennedy then went on to recount two lesser known efforts that were typical of Yarborough's deep concern for people. One was about the Senator's work in September 1961 to obtain urgently needed White House backing to help bring aid to Texas' Gulf Coast when Hurricane Carla spawned terrible devastation and human suffering. The second concerned Yarborough's long fight for enactment of legislation to establish a National Seashore Recreation Area on Padre Island, providing facilities for all citizens to enjoy their leisure amidst its natural beauty.

Historical Shadows

Such a tribute illustrates one of the most remarkable aspects of Ralph Yarborough's career—his ability to stake out his own independent courses of action in the Senate in

Participants at planning session for 1968 Hemisphere Exposition in San Antonio, Texas were Senator Yarborough, Congressman Henry B. Gonzales of San Antonio and County Judge Charles W. Grace.

Surprising reception for Senator Yarborough in April 1968 when he addressed Texas State Council Convention of the Retail Clerks Union, AFL-CIO in Fort Worth.

order to bring such a range of benefits to people who are most in need of assistance that governmental policies can provide.

During his first twelve years of Senate service, Yarborough worked in the shadow of a far more renowned Texan—Lyndon Baines Johnson. Both Yarborough and Johnson were strongly motivated to use government programs for the benefit of the "common man." When they were in agreement—which was often—it was not newsworthy; when they disagreed it attracted notice and was unrealistically magnified.

The accidents of history made it inevitable that Yarborough would be, in sequence, the junior Senator from the home State of the Senate's Majority Leader—the senior Senator from the Vice President's home State—and finally, the senior Senator from the President's State of Texas. To say that Senator Yarborough held a preempted position in the Senate for virtually all of his first twelve years there is an ironic understatement. But despite the relative news eclipse that shrouded most of his diligent legislative activities, he succeeded in creating his own leadership position in the Senate during this tumultuous period. Today, Chairman Ralph Yarborough is publicized little but known well by the more knowledgeable Washington reporters.

Yarborough and the Media

The partial Yarborough "news blackout," includes both the national press and many Texas newspapers, but Yarborough still manages to keep in close touch with the people of Texas. Like most Senators, he regularly issues a legislative newsletter—"Ralph Yarborough's Washington Report." His correspondence with Texans is measured not by letter-count, but by numbers of full mail bags. He hopefully sends out periodic press releases to describe his Senate activities—and is grateful if the news is printed by some Texas papers. He tapes regular radio reports that are sometimes carried by more than 100 radio stations throughout the State. He occasionally tapes a TV report for showing during public service times. Whenever the pressures of his Senate duties will permit, Yarborough jets down to Texas, squeezes in as many speaking engagements as he can, meets and talks with as many Texans as possible. He has kept up this full schedule of personal contacts despite his heavy workload as Chairman of the Labor and Public Welfare Committee.

The Eyes of Texas
Election—1970 and the Future

Election year 1970 will be the acid test of the viability of the Yarborough "coalition" of "just people, no big shots." It will try the faith that the Senator places in the sound political judgment and economic common sense of the people of Texas. Senator Ralph Yarborough and 23 other Democratic colleagues in the Senate are taking their records of public stewardship to their respective electorates for approval.

The people of the big Lone Star Nation-State, as well as the people of the United States as a whole, have a vital stake in how the Texas voters judge Senator Ralph Webster Yarborough's twelve-year record of service in their behalf. His future in the Senate and his leadership role as Chairman of the Labor and Public Welfare Committee will be laid on the line.

Texans may well remember the message of John F. Kennedy on that October, 1963 night in Austin:

"This is a time for all of us who believe in government for the people, who believe in progress for our country, who believe in a fair chance for all of our citizens, who believe in the growth of Texas, who believe in a United States which is second to none in space, on the sea, on the land, a United States which stands for progress—all of those—I think Ralph Yarborough stands with them."

Senator Yarborough is shown with Austin Photographer Russell Lee at the opening of Lee's Photography Exhibition at the Smithsonian Museum in Washington. (Picture in background was taken by Russell Lee during Senator Yarborough's 1964 campaign.)

Acknowledgments

The author gratefully acknowledges the use of the special series of photographs by Russell Lee of Austin, Texas. In as many cases as possible, other pictures that have greatly enhanced the book are also identified and credited below.

Much valuable time was provided by Senator Yarborough to the author for interviews. The assistance of his able staff in furnishing research materials, election data, picture identification and other helpful information is likewise deeply appreciated.

The author is similarly grateful for the use of information contained in the photo-biography entitled *Yarborough—Portrait of a People's Senator,* by Mark Adams and Creekmore Fath, published in 1957 by The Chaparral Press, Austin, Texas.

Finally acknowledged is the editorial assistance provided by Alan Hall, whose efforts were so important to the successful completion of this book.

This book cannot be considered as a definitive work on the public career of Senator Ralph W. Yarborough, whose wide-ranging activities in the Senate could fill many volumes. Nor can such a book begin to mention the important political roles played by the thousands of loyal campaign workers and supporters, whose efforts have contributed so much to the progressive changes in Texas politics. Acknowledging these substantive limitations, the author likewise bears full responsibility for statements, observations and opinions expressed herein.

The quotation from John Gunther's *Inside U.S.A.* used on page 44, copyright 1947, is used by permission of Harper & Row, Publishers, Incorporated, New York.

PICTURE CREDITS:

Photographs on front and back covers and photographs on Pages 10, 16, 32, 52, 56, 67, 69, 70, 72, 74, 90, 126, 129 and 135 are by Russell Lee. Others are: Title Page, 1964 Campaign Night Rally at the Alamo, San Antonio. Photo by Mike Cantu, Page 19, Merkle Press; Page 39, The *Suburban Journal*; Page 41, From *Yarborough—Portrait of a People's Senator* by Adams and Fath, The Chaparral Press, Austin, Texas; Page 48, World Wide Photos, Inc.; Page 61, Dallas *Morning News* staff photo; Page 78, Ira Mandelbaum, Scope Associates; Page 99, White House photo; Page 103, Cartoon by Herc Ficklen, Dallas *Morning News*. Used with permission; Page 106, Ira Mandelbaum, Scope Associates; Page 107, FDA photo; Page 108, U.S. Army Photograph, U.S. Darnall Army Hospital, Fort Hood, Texas; Page 115 (top) The Methodist Hospital, Texas Medical Center, Houston, Texas; Page 119, White House photo; Page 122, White House photo; Page 132, Dallas Chamber of Commerce; Page 134, U.S. Army Photograph; Page 136, White House photo; Page 137, Iran Press Photographers Association; Page 139, Capitol Photo Service, Inc.; Page 142, NASA—National Aeronautics and Space Administration photo; Page 143, Christopher Studio, Beaumont, Texas; Page 153, Harichrome Studio, San Antonio, Texas; Page 154, Squire Haskins Photo, Dallas, Texas; Page 157, The Smithsonian Institution.

Appendix

Senator Yarborough has received an unusually high number of honors, awards, citations, medals, plaques, scrolls and other tangible symbols of excellence for his legislative achievements. They occupy prominent positions on the walls of his Senate offices. Among the scores of such awards, a few listed below provide insight into the broad range they encompass.

Doctor of Humane Letters (honorary), Lincoln College, Lincoln Illinois (1965)

Honorary Fellow, Postgraduate Center for Mental Health, New York (1965)

Honorary Citizen, County of Los Angeles, California (1968)

Honorary Fellow, International College of Dentists (1969)

Honorary Membership, Texas Library Association

Honorary Life Membership, Texas Association for Retarded Children

Trustee, Kennedy Center for the Performing Arts

Former Member, Executive Board, Civil War Centennial Commission

Former Member, Lincoln Sesquicentennial Commission

Member, Board of Directors, Gallaudet College, Washington, D. C. (1969)

National Director, National Rivers and Harbors Congress

Member, Active Board of Trustees, U.S. Capitol Historical Society

Member, Board of Visitors, U.S. Naval Academy

About the Author ───────

William G. Phillips is an experienced political figure on the Washington scene who has observed the important leadership role of Senator Ralph W. Yarborough since the Texan was elected to the Senate in 1957.

A veteran staff member of the House of Representatives since 1955, Phillips served as Administrative Assistant to former Representative George M. Rhodes of Pennsylvania. He was the first Staff Director of the Democratic Study Group in the House from 1959 through 1965.

In 1966 he was appointed Assistant Director of the Office of Economic Opportunity, Executive Office of the President, where he was in charge of Congressional Relations for the anti-poverty program.

Later, he served as Deputy Chairman (Research) of the Democratic National Committee before entering private business in legislative counseling and public relations. In July, 1969 he was named Staff Director of the Special Labor Subcommittee, Education and Labor Committee in the House of Representatives.

Phillips is a native of Charleroi, Pennsylvania and a World War II veteran. He received his B.A. and M.A. degrees in political science from The American University, Washington, D.C. An expert on the legislative process, he is the author of *Operation: Congress*, as well as numerous articles on Congress, public affairs and related fields.